The ARMCHAIR MAGICIAN

Dr. Barbara L. Thaw & Stephen J. Ronson

A Dell Trade Paperback

A DELL TRADE PAPERBACK

Published by
Dell Publishing
a division of
Bantam Doubleday Dell Publishing Group, Inc.
1540 Broadway
New York, New York 10036

Library of Congress Cataloging in Publication Data
Thaw, Barbara L.
    The armchair magician/Barbara L. Thaw & Stephen J. Ronson.
        p. cm.
    Includes bibliographical references.
    ISBN 0-440-50671-9
    1. Conjuring. 2. Conjuring—History. 3. Tricks. Magicians—Biography. I. Ronson, Stephen J.
II. Title.
GV1547. T43 1994
793.8 dc20   94—5766
                                                    CIP

Printed in the United States of America
Published simultaneously in Canada
November 1994

10 9 8 7 6 5 4 3 2 1

Book produced by **David Kaestle, Inc.**
Art director: **David Kaestle**
Designer: **Richard DeMonico**
Instructional illustrations: **William Ruggieri**
Cartoon illustrations: **John Caldwell**
Cover illustration: **Bill Purdom**

Special thanks to Christie Sherman for her reference photography and to Stephen Ronson for his enthusiastic cooperation throughout two tedious photo sessions.

Contents

Dedications

We dedicate this book to our parents, Christine, Golda and Irving, who, to this day, still ask, "Is that a trick deck?"
We also dedicate this book to Mario Gonzalez, a true magician and a true friend, and to the memory of Frank Garcia, the Man with the Million-Dollar Hands.

Thank-You's

Special thanks to our editor and friend Tony Gangi, whose great enthusiasm and expertise made this book possible.

We'd also like to say thank-you to Millie and Lenny Thaw for teaching us how to turn a computer on and off, and to Christine Duggan, Mike Duggan, and Irving Gonzalez for their invaluable input. Sincere appreciation to Julie Marchione, Luci Lamster, and Eddie Morton for their support throughout the years.

Thanks to Harry Blackstone, Jr., for contributing the photo of his father, the great Harry Blackstone, Sr.

And finally, a very personal thank-you to Siegfried and Roy, the most spectacular stage illusionists of our day.

The field of magic has historically been dominated by men, but included in the roster of names are lesser-known great women performers.

Today, almost as many girls as boys are attracted to magic as a hobby and from there move forward into professional performing careers.

It is only for the sake of simplicity and consistency that we refer to the magician as "he" throughout this book.

Foreword

"How do you make an elephant disappear?"..."How do you change a lady into a white tiger?"... "How do the two of you change places in a split second?"...

The questions are always the same and our answer never varies.

First of all, you need to invoke a magic word! In our case, we simply say, "SARMOTI." That stands for "Siegfried & Roy, Masters of the Impossible."

Of course, that is where we try to end the conversation. But there always are those for whom the answer is insufficient. These are the ones who will go to the ends of the earth in a relentless quest to lay their hands on the sacred tome containing *all* the secrets of magic. But there is no *one* illusion, no *one* philosophy, no *one* sacred scroll that will transform a person into a magician. But you do have to start somewhere. And that somewhere is here and in the pages to follow.

The Armchair Magician will put you on the road toward learning some of the essentials of this fascinating art.

After years of perfecting our skills, we can make tigers and elephants disappear; we can levitate ladies, then change them into wild cheetahs. But you cannot begin learning to be a magician with tigers and elephants in Las Vegas. One must have humble beginnings. For many of you, *The Armchair Magician* will be that humble beginning.

We are pleased to encourage a new generation of aspiring magical artists. May the spirit of SARMOTI be with you throughout your adventures in illusion!

Magically yours,

Siegfried & Roy

Before the Show

The Armchair Magician proposes to profoundly change your beliefs about magic. We propose to teach you what magic really is, and why it works. With a little practice and a lot of enthusiasm, you will be performing miracles right in your own living room, while sitting in the comfort of your easy chair.

To the layman, magic is enshrouded in an impenetrable cloud of mystery. To clear the smoke, to break through, we'll need to closely examine some of our misconceptions, the fallacies, the perpetuated rumors that serve to shield and protect the *real* secrets of this ancient craft.

COMMON FALLACIES

"The hand is quicker than the eye."

No, it is not. The eye reacts far more quickly than the hand is able to move.

"Hey, it's up his sleeve!"

Not usually. Only one out of one hundred tricks might involve hiding an object up the magician's sleeve.

"I know how it's done. It has something to do with mirrors."

As rarely as a magician hides something up his sleeve, even less frequently does he create his illusions with mirrors.

"I could never do that. I'm not good with my hands."

As you will find, magic does not require dexterity. It requires learning the art of misdirection, which is applied psychology.

NOW PUT IT BACK IN THE DECK, ANYWHERE!

"It's a trick deck."

True, some effects require special packs of cards. But many of the best miracles are performed with ordinary, ungimmicked decks.

We're left with one simple question: **How do magicians fool us?**

We all like to think of ourselves as intelligent, observant adults — at least regarding what is possible and what is not. And yet, when we witness a well-executed trick, we're awestruck; despite our beliefs, we feel we've witnessed the impossible. We assume the trick must have been done by complicated and elaborate means. How else could we possibly have been fooled? But the plain truth is this: *The smarter the man, the easier he is to fool*. We live in an intricate world; our brains are filled with complex information and ideas. The more information we take in and the smarter we become, the less likely we are to attribute obvious causes to mystifying effects.

But there's yet another dimension to the baffling question of why we're so easily fooled, and the key lies in the very marrow of the craft. The magician does, indeed, have something hidden up his sleeve. It's intangible, invisible — but without it, his efforts would come to naught. He is armed with a working knowledge of the principles of human nature and behavior. His understanding of these principles and his ability to apply them are his primary tools in performing what appears to be the impossible.

When your uncle vanished a coin from the palm of his hand and then pulled it from your ear, he was invoking the same principle as Houdini when he vanished a two-ton elephant onstage in 1918. The scale is different; the principles are the same. Nothing in magic is left to chance. *Human nature is predictable*. **Magicians take advantage of human nature to ply their craft**.

THE PRINCIPLES

or

What's Really Up the Magician's Sleeve

Principle #1
FALSE ASSUMPTION

The spectator assumes the magician is telling the truth.

A casketlike box is rolled onstage. The magician opens the lid, takes the hand of his elegant assistant, and guides her as she steps into the box. She lies down inside it, her head, hands, and lower quarter of her legs protruding. The magician places her in a trance, closes the lid, and throws a switch. A powerful buzz saw descends, cuts the box in two, and severs the woman's body. The two halves of the box are separated and pushed to opposite sides of the stage. The toes wriggle, the disembodied head smiles. The boxes are reunited. The lid is opened and the woman emerges, healthy and whole.

Supporting the magician's use of all the principles of magic — which you will be introduced to — is the spectator's overwhelming tendency to take for granted that the magician is doing exactly what he says he is doing — that what the spectator sees with his own eyes is the whole story, when, in fact, he has been shown only a very few details and has logically filled in the blanks all by himself. This blatant satisfaction with only a part of the story, which the spectator takes to represent the whole, is often the sole operating principle that enables the magician to create his seemingly impossible effects.

False Assumption...Did anyone step forward and declare that the wriggling toes actually belonged to the elegant assistant? No one said they were hers. No one said they weren't.

MISDIRECTION

The magician draws attention away from the trick zone, for an instant, so that an unexplained move can be invisibly made.

There are two basic types of misdirection.

Visual Misdirection:

The spectator will always look where the magician looks.

Richard Cardini (1896–1973) was best known for producing endless quantities of lit cigarettes and pipes, one after the other, from apparently empty hands. The cigarettes and pipes were all hidden on his person, but how did he retrieve them without being caught? Mr. Cardini customarily did his secret move when his beautiful assistant, Swan, walked onstage. All eyes darted toward her as she entered, and the magician, unobserved, would obtain the hidden props, conceal them in his palms, and produce the items one by one by one.

The magician often takes advantage of his own natural, habitual, and repeated movements to casually draw attention away from the trick zone without arousing suspicion. He looks at, and reaches for, the cigarette he is smoking. He adjusts his eyeglasses. Unconsciously, the spectator's eyes follow the magician's; the spectator pays attention to whatever the magician seems to be paying attention to. Even if he's distracted his audience for only a second, he's given himself enough time to do whatever he needs to do to execute an action with the other, unobserved, hand.

Mental Misdirection:

The human mind will concentrate on only one thing at a given time.

A spectator is asked to pick a card from the deck and memorize it. He has been given a simple task, one that will occupy him for only a fraction of a second. But it's in this brief moment of distraction that the magician is free to make his secret move. He switches decks, or cuts the deck, or adds cards, or takes cards away, or palms one or two from the bottom to the top.

Asking the spectator his name would have had the same effect. The magician accomplishes his goal, distracting his spectator's mind.

CONCEALMENT

The magician is able to hide a vital piece of information, because the spectator won't look for what he doesn't expect to see.

Either a prepared gimmick or the bare hand, precisely positioned, can be used to conceal a piece of information. A most dramatic example of the Concealment principle can be observed with the simple "thumb tip," a prop included with this book, which is used to make small objects like cigarettes, silks, or salt appear and vanish. Some time ago, when we first began our study of magic, our instructor introduced us to the fake-looking thumb tip, and naturally, we were skeptical about its ability to fool anybody with a pair of eyes. But when he performed a trick for us, using the device, we could not, no matter what, no matter how hard we tried, actually see it on our mentor's hand. It remained invisible.

In subsequent years we experimented with odd, boldly colored tips, to challenge the Concealment principle.... Not even one of our spectators saw anything out of the ordinary on our hands; they remained baffled by our "magical" prowess, as yours will be with yours.

Principle #4
MAGICIAN'S CHOICE OR FORCING

The spectator believes he is being given free choice, but the outcome has been predetermined.

In 1846 Robert-Houdin, who is considered to be the father of modern magic, was summoned to the court of King Louis Philippe, where he performed what was to become one of his most baffling and memorable feats.

The magician collected handkerchiefs belonging to six of the noblemen in his audience and placed them beneath an opaque glass dome. Robert-Houdin then approached the king and presented him with a handful of cards, each bearing the name of a different location. The king selected a card that read "The chest beneath the last tree on the right, in the orange grove." Robert-Houdin lifted the glass dome, and the handkerchiefs had vanished. He directed the king's servants to leave the palace and dig at the base of the chosen tree, where they did, indeed, find a buried chest. Locked and rusted, it was placed before the king. The magician handed the king a key, and the box was opened. Inside, the king found an old parchment dated 1786, written by the deceased, but still famous conjurer Cagliostro, which stated that he, himself, had placed the iron box with the handkerchiefs at the base of the selected tree to serve in the performance of an act of magic to be executed sixty years later. The chest contained not only the parchment but a sealed envelope in which were found the six handkerchiefs borrowed just a few minutes earlier from the king's men.

The king attributed the outcome to witchcraft, but Robert-Houdin had utilized the principle of Magician's Choice or Forcing. The king, in taking the card naming the orange grove location, believed that it was his own free selection, but it was not. The magician had decided, in advance, which card he needed the king to take, and had forced it on him, without the king ever realizing it or suspecting it. Prior to presentation, the iron chest lay in waiting in a hole in the ground. The noblemen's handkerchiefs were secretly given to the magician's assistant, who deposited them in the chest with the letter. Back in the palace, the king was choosing the preselected card, and Robert-Houdin was well on his way to performing the incomprehensible.

There are many principles involved in a magician's performance. We've introduced you to what we feel are the most basic principles, the most widely used, the most crucial to understand. We believe that the application of these principles is one of the most profound and fascinating aspects of the craft, but the principles, by themselves, are only part of the story. To perform what appears to be a miracle, you will also need to know what to say, how to say it, and why.

22

A FEW WORDS ABOUT PATTER

Patter refers to the stories told, the explanations offered, all statements made by the magician during the performance of an effect.

Some patter consists of serious or exotic tales; some magicians speak in poetic metaphor. Others use light gags and one-liners. Some prefer the straightforward approach and explain only what they are doing and what is about to happen.

In fact, much of the magician's patter is his way of directing his audience's attention exactly where he wants it. When he opens his mouth to speak, his audience momentarily looks away from his hands and toward his face, concentrating on his words and not his actions. With his patter he can allay his audience's suspicions by providing convincing reasons for any unnatural moves he needs to make. He can stimulate their imaginations and lead them in the direction he wishes to take them, away from the path of the commonplace, expected, and logical.

The patter has yet another use: It can be utilized to create a Time Delay between the execution of a critical move and the surprising final outcome of the trick. The spectator will not only disregard the magician's natural, unsuspicious, and seemingly unimportant move, but the lapse of time and the intervening patter will make him entirely forget that it ever even happened!

There is only one rule to strictly adhere to when creating patter: *Keep it interesting*. How? Like everything we've exposed to you about the underlying fundamentals of magic, this, too, is so obvious, so simple, it borders on absurdity. Your audience will only be as interested as you are. Be amazed and they, too, will be amazed. Keep in mind that you are an actor, playing the role of a magician. Experiment. Find a style you're comfortable with, a style that sounds natural and unrehearsed. It won't happen immediately; a style evolves over the course of time. Be willing to surprise yourself. Many a would-be magician has pictured himself as the rehearsed storytelling type only to discover inside a gift for the comic, the blunt, or the spontaneous.

We've provided examples of suggested patter for many of the effects that follow. Although they will each work appropriately in actual performance, they'd best be taken as simple examples of how to think about patter, as diagrammatic representations of how words, stories, and explanations can work in tandem with physical actions. Think about the events of your own life, your philosophies, dilemmas, dreams. Magic has a different meaning to each of us. *Your* meaning will be reflected in the patter *you* create.

MEANING, SHMEANING!

"IT'S SHOWTIME"

Okay, you're sitting comfortably in your easy chair. The dog's been walked, the kids are in bed. Now it's time to sit back and relax into an exciting and wonderful new hobby, rich with age-old tradition and long-guarded secrets, admired and adored by ancient civilizations, all from the comfort of your living room. You are on your way to becoming a master magician, a great conjurer, an expert in legerdemain, a swift and sly sleight-of-hand artist. Okay, that's stretching it a bit, but you will come away with some easy-to-do feats of hocus-pocus that will amaze your friends and family. Let's take a quick peek at the program....

THE CATEGORIES OF MAGIC

or

What Magicians Do

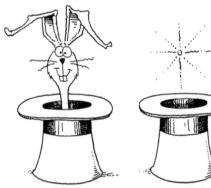

PRODUCTION...
An object
suddenly appears.

VANISH...
An object
suddenly
disappears.

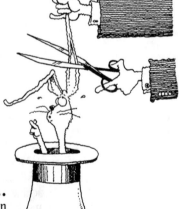

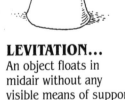

RESTORATION...
An object is destroyed and is then
restored to its original form.

LEVITATION...
An object floats in
midair without any
visible means of support.

PENETRATION...
One solid object moves
through another.

TRANSPOSITION...
An object moves from one place to another, or objects change places.

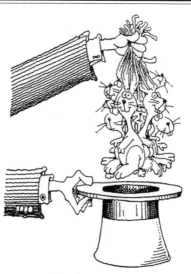

MULTIPLICATION...
A single object duplicates itself.

REVELATION...
Any effect that culminates with a highly improbable but interesting outcome.

TRANSFORMATION...
One object turns into another.

MENTALISM...
Any effect that is achieved by what appears to be superior mental ability.

THE EFFECTS

In the following chapter, we will take you slowly through twenty-five magic effects. For each trick, we've identified the main principle it embodies, the category it belongs to, and all props used. Although each effect is titled, this is for your eyes only. Never introduce a trick to your spectator by using its name; the effect, the surprise ending, would be greatly diminished.

Are you ready? The curtain's about to go up.

The ARMCHAIR MAGICIAN

Seven amazing feats of illusion
based on the first principle of magic

FALSE ASSUMPTION

Category
Revelation

Prop
One deck of cards

EFFECT

The magician takes a deck of cards, does a hand spread, and asks the spectator to freely select any card. The spectator is asked to remember his chosen card and, without revealing it to the magician, to place it back anywhere in the deck. The magician squares the deck neatly, showing the spectator that there are no breaks, no marks of any kind. The card is clearly lost in the deck. The magician places the deck behind his back for a fraction of a second. He once again brings the deck out in front, spreads the cards face-down, and reveals to the spectator that his secret chosen card has indeed been found: it is the only face-up card in the deck.

SET-UP

Before the deck is introduced, prior to presentation, take the bottom card (in our example the Jack of Clubs), and turn it face-up, leaving it on the bottom of the deck (**fig. 1**).

METHOD

Take your prepared deck of cards, face-down, and do a hand spread. Be careful not to expose the bottom card, i.e., the Jack of Clubs. Ask the spectator to freely select any card. Tell him to memorize his chosen card. As he pulls the card from the deck and momentarily occupies himself with this task, secretly and naturally turn the deck over so that the bottom card (the Jack of Clubs) is now the top card. At this point, unknown to the spectator, only the top card is face-down and the rest of the deck is face-up. Seeing the top face-down card, the spectator falsely assumes that all the cards are face-down. Ask the spectator to now place his chosen card, face-down, back into the deck **(fig. 2)**.

Square the deck. Show the spectator that there are no breaks, no marks, no way whatsoever for you to know what card he chose or where exactly it now is. Take the squared deck in one hand, place it behind your back. As you pass the deck from one hand to the other, reverse the deck once again so that the deck is in its original orientation. (All the cards are again face-down except the Jack of Clubs.) In front of the spectator do a hand-to-hand spread of the apparently face-down deck, again being careful not to reveal that bottom card. The spectator's secret card appears to be the only face-up card in the deck **(fig. 3)**.

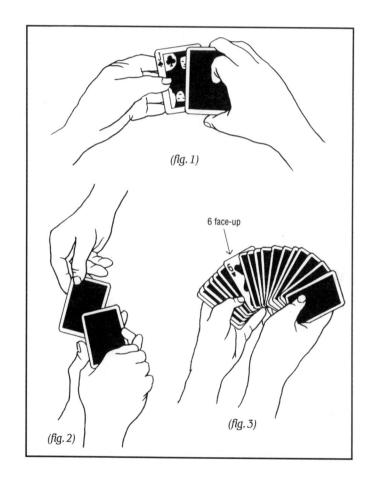

(fig. 1)

6 face-up

(fig. 2)

(fig. 3)

THE COLOR-CHANGING THIMBLE

Category
Transformation

Props
Two thimbles — one red, one blue

EFFECT

The magician places a red thimble on his fingertip. He shakes his hand up and down and instantly the red thimble changes to a blue one. He shakes his hand again and it changes back to red.

SET-UP

Take the blue thimble and place it on the tip of the middle finger of either hand. Position your hand so your pinky is closest to the spectator. Loosely curl your fingers so that the pinkie, ring finger, and the middle finger with the blue thimble are now hidden in your palm (**fig. 1**).

METHOD

In front of your spectator, place the red thimble on the pointer finger of the same hand in which you've hidden the blue one. Rest the tip of your pointer, with the red thimble, on the tip of the thumb. In this position rapidly shake your hand up and down (**fig. 2**). While in motion, switch your middle finger for your pointer, so that the middle finger with the blue thimble is now resting on your thumb and the pointer with the red thimble is curled into your palm (**fig. 3**). Shake your hand again and switch the hidden pointer with the middle finger. The spectator will always falsely assume that the finger they are currently seeing is the same one they saw before.

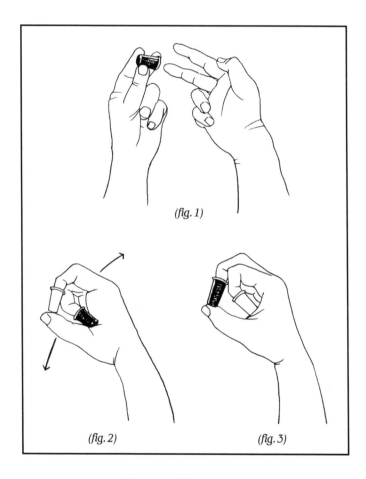

(fig. 1)

(fig. 2)   (fig. 3)

ALWAYS BE PREPARED....
MAX MALINI (1875–1942)

When dining at elegant restaurants, Max Malini would borrow a gentleman's hat and, to the amazement of the waiter and his companions, would produce a large block of ice from under it. He became well known for this humorous stunt, but as with all magic, the impossible is rendered possible with a little preparation, a little misdirection, and a little well-kept secret. Malini always went out to dine with a block of ice concealed under his dinner jacket and held in place with a pair of tongs. When just the right moment and situation presented itself, the conjurer caused the block to suddenly appear. If the correct situation and timing didn't happen, if his potential audience could not be suitably misdirected, the trick remained unrevealed and Malini would return home dripping wet.

THE COINCIDENTAL CUT

Category
Revelation

Prop
One deck of cards

EFFECT

The magician hands the spectator a deck of cards and invites him to shuffle it thoroughly. The spectator is then asked to cut the deck, to look at the card he has cut to, and without revealing it to the magician, to replace it in the deck. The spectator completes the cut, thereby losing the card within the deck. The magician takes the deck, and just as the spectator has done, he cuts the deck, memorizes the card he has cut to, and completes the cut. Both the spectator and the magician reveal their chosen card to one another. Against all odds, when the deck is exposed face-up, the spectator's card and the magician's card are found right next to one another in the deck.

SET-UP

This effect is repeatable and requires no prior set-up.

METHOD

Hand an unprepared face-down deck of cards to the spectator. Ask him to shuffle the deck. When, to his satisfaction, they are shuffled, momentarily take the deck back from him. As you do so, secretly and casually take note of the bottom card — the Jack of Clubs in our example — and memorize it. Place the deck face-down in front of the spectator. Ask him to cut the deck in half. You now have two piles of cards. Pile A is the top half. Pile B is the bottom half, with the Jack of Clubs as the bottom card **(fig. 1)**.

Ask the spectator to look at the card he has cut to, the top card of Pile B. Ask him to remember this card, to place it on top of Pile A, and to "complete the cut" by placing all of Pile B on top of Pile A **(fig. 2)**.

Now you, too, will do exactly what the spectator has just done, with one exception. You will cut the deck into two piles, look at the card you cut to, the top card of Pile B, place this card on top of Pile A, and complete the cut by placing all of Pile B on top of Pile A. The exception is that, unbeknownst to the spectator, although you have looked at the card you cut to, you are only *pretending* to memorize it. This card is secretly disregarded; it has nothing to do with the trick.

Ask the spectator to reveal the name of his chosen card. But the card *you* reveal to him, the card you name, is not the card you've just cut to, but rather, the card you initially memorized at the bottom of the deck, the Jack of Clubs. (The spectator falsely assumes you are telling the truth, that you are doing exactly what you say you are). Turn the deck face-up. Your named card and the spectator's card are miraculously found side by side in the deck **(fig. 3)**.

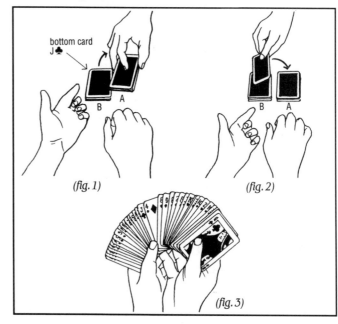

bottom card
J♣

(fig. 1)

(fig. 2)

(fig. 3)

COIN THROUGH TABLE

Category
Penetration

Props
Two quarters or two half dollars, one dinner table

EFFECT

While sitting at a dinner table the magician announces, "Did you know that there is a 'soft spot' in every table? I'd like to try to find it." He reaches into his pocket and produces a coin. The magician shows his left hand is empty and places it under the table. With his right hand, he picks up the coin and gently slaps it onto the table. "This is not the soft spot," he says. The magician picks up the coin and slaps it down in a different area, again declaring his failure to find the correct spot.

One more time the coin is slapped down onto the tabletop. The spectator hears the slight click of the coin as it meets the table's surface. "Ah," the magician says, "here is the soft spot!" The magician presses his palm down upon the table and rubs the tabletop in a circular motion. He lifts his right hand; the coin has vanished. "But," the magician informs the spectator, "the coin has not really vanished. It has merely passed through the soft spot in the table." He brings his left hand out from under the table, reveals the coin and says, "Would you please pass the mashed potatoes?"

SET-UP

Prior to presentation, choose which coin you'd like to use, quarters or half dollars. In our example, we'll choose the quarters.

While sitting at the table, secretly place one quarter on your left knee. Let a few minutes pass before you announce that you will attempt to find the soft spot.

METHOD

Reach into your pocket with your right hand and take out a quarter. Allow your spectator to examine the coin **(fig. 1)**. Show your left hand is empty and place it under the tabletop. Here's your secret move. As you reach beneath the table, secretly pick up the quarter which is sitting, unseen, on your left knee. Rest your left hand, with the hidden coin, palm up, against the bottom side of the table. You are now ready to begin your "search" for the soft spot.

With your right hand, gently slap the quarter that you've taken from your pocket down upon the tabletop. Inform the spectator that you have not located the correct spot; the coin still lies visibly on the table. In a sliding motion, drag the coin across the top of the table, right to the edge where

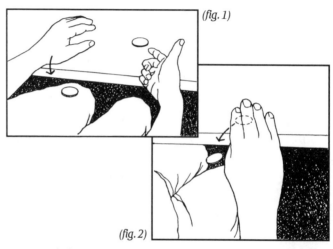

(fig. 1)

(fig. 2)

you are sitting. Now pick it up off the table. You will repeat this exact sequence twice. On your third attempt to locate the soft spot, you will make your next secret move. Drag the coin to the table's edge, as before, but this time, allow it to fall down onto your lap **(fig. 2)**. The importance of presenting two failed attempts now becomes evident. You must accustom your spectator to the dragging motion you employ when picking up the coin. It will begin to look dramatic, not odd. Then, when you secretly dispose of the coin onto your lap, the motion you use will be exactly the same motion you used twice before, and therefore it will not arouse suspicion. So, remember, each and every time you slap down the coin, you must pick it up by sliding it across the table to the edge.

On what appears to be your fourth attempt, pretend that you still have the coin in your right hand, and slap it down onto the table, as before. To convince the spectator that the coin is still in your hand, slap the underside of the table with the hidden coin in your left hand. The clicking sound will convince your spectator that nothing unusual has, as yet, happened. Now announce that you have finally found the table's soft spot. Pretend to rub the quarter into the table, until it vanishes. Remove your right hand from the table, and reveal that the coin is gone. Bring your left hand, with the hidden quarter, out from underneath the table. The coin appears to have penetrated the solid dinner table.

TIPS

We've just introduced you to a popular and favorite technique of many professional magicians. When any small object is secretly disposed of onto the magician's lap, it is known as "lapping." Tony Slydini, born in Argentina, was considered to be one of the greatest close-up magicians that the field has ever known. He truly reaped the benefits of lapping in performing his effects, elevating the technique to an art in itself.

• Lapping needs to be executed in a very casual manner. But it is your prior repetitive movements that really allow the secret move to pass undetected.

• It is vital to remember that you need to do nothing more or less than slide the coin to the edge a few times before dropping it onto your lap. We feel that three unsuccessful attempts work best; there is no need to do more than three, as it will become tedious to your spectator.

• When getting ready to lap your coin, keep your knees together so that the coin doesn't fall onto the floor; the noise of the dropping coin may give away the trick. Sitting at a dinner table also gives you a good excuse to have your napkin across your lap; the napkin makes a great catching device!

• Experiment. You may find that you're able to lap other small objects besides a coin — a finger ring, salt shaker, even a deck of cards....

Category
Mentalism

Props
One deck of cards, one business card (borrowed or your own)

EFFECT

The magician borrows a business card from his spectator, turns it over, and writes a prediction on its back. The magician then conceals the prediction by turning over the business card, the printed side now facing up. The magician presents an ordinary face-down deck of cards and asks the spectator to insert the business card anywhere into the deck. The prediction remains concealed. The magician thumbs through the deck until he reaches the inserted business card and asks the spectator if he is satisfied with his decision, or if he would like to change his mind.

When the spectator claims that he is satisfied, the magician then says,"I want to show you that I did actually write something on the back of your card; I don't want you to think that I was only pretending to. I'm going to quickly show you the back of your business card, but too quickly for you to actually read it." The magician does exactly as he has said, proving that there is clearly something handwritten on the back. The magician goes on to remind the spectator that all was fair, that he could have placed the card anywhere at all in the deck.

The magician asks the spectator to remove his business card from the deck, along with the playing card immediately before it and the playing card immediately after it. The spectator now holds three cards: two playing cards with one business card sandwiched between them. The spectator is now asked to turn over the business card, and for the first time, to read the magician's prediction. He is then instructed to turn over the two playing cards. The written prediction states the value of two playing cards; the magician has correctly predicted exactly where in the deck the spectator would choose to place his business card.

SET-UP

This set-up can be done either prior to presentation or, with a little misdirection, right in front of the spectator.

Glance at and remember both the top card and the bottom card of your deck.

METHOD

In our example, the top card of the deck is the King of Hearts, the bottom card is the Two of Clubs.

Borrow a business card from the spectator, turn it over, and proceed to write the following prediction on its back: "You will choose the King of Hearts and the Two of Clubs." Do not allow the spectator to see what you are writing; turn the business card over, printed side up, the prediction concealed.

Hand the business card back to the spectator and ask him, without looking at the prediction, to insert it somewhere into the middle of your deck of playing cards **(fig. 1)**. Square up the deck so that the business card is now clearly lost within it. Thumb through the deck, stopping when you come to the business card, its printed side facing up. Offer the spectator a chance to change his mind about where he's chosen to place it. If he opts to change its placement, allow him to, merely repeating the steps that immediately follow your writing of the prediction. This trick relies mostly on the principle of Time Delay, so you will now need to do a little bit of talking, which we will help you with as we go along.

Explain to the spectator that you wish to prove to him that you did indeed write something on the back of his card. But this patter is merely an excuse that will allow you to execute a move that will change the placement of his card without his knowing. When done smoothly and casually, the simple move is extremely deceptive. In your right hand, gather up all the cards that are on top of the

business card. You are now holding the top half of the deck in your right hand. Your left hand holds the bottom half of the deck, with the business card lying printed side up, on

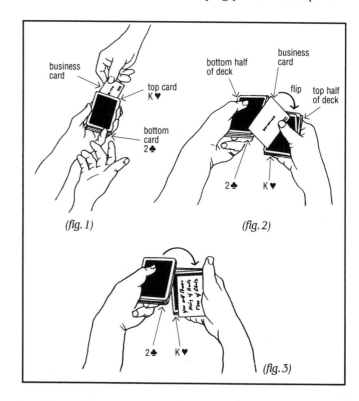

(fig. 1)

(fig. 2)

(fig. 3)

top of it. Using your left thumb, flip the business card over onto the top card of the top half of the deck in your right hand. Immediately drop the bottom half of the deck, the portion in your left hand, onto the business card and deck in your right hand **(fig. 2)**. If you take a close look you'll see that the business card is now sandwiched between the King of Hearts and the Two of Clubs, the two cards we took note of in the set-up — the top and bottom cards of the deck **(fig. 3)**.

You will have to practice this move so that it begins to appear as though you are merely flipping over the business card. During this move and just after it, the patter supporting the Time Delay becomes very important, allowing the spectator to forget where, exactly, he actually placed his card. Your patter will consist of reinforcing for the spectator, over and over, certain simple ideas. For example, "So you see, I have actually written something on your card, I wasn't pretending.... You weren't able to read it, were you? I could not possibly have known where you'd place the card," etc.

Finally, tell the spectator to remove the business card from the face-down deck, taking along with it the playing card lying immediately before it and the card lying immediately after it. He now holds his business card, sandwiched between two playing cards. For the first time, allow the spectator to read your prediction and then to turn over the two correctly predicted adjacent playing cards.

TIPS

• To assure that your secret maneuver remains invisible, ask the spectator, when you begin the effect, to place his card somewhere into the middle portion of the deck.

• You might want to carry small index cards with you in the event that neither you nor the spectator has a business card.

• If the spectator should opt to change the position of his business card in the deck, it's always entertaining to suggest to him that you had a strong feeling that he would change his mind; thank him for doing so, or else the trick would not have worked! Bringing something mysterious to a trick is always very impressive.

• In aiming to make your Time Delay effective, it's okay to be somewhat repetitive with your patter. Your repetition can serve to dramatize just how fair everything is....

TWIN MIRACLE

Category
Revelation

Props
Two decks of cards — one blue-backed, one red-backed

EFFECT

The magician presents two decks of cards — one red, one blue. The spectator is asked to select one of the decks, the magician picks up the other. Both the magician and the spectator thoroughly shuffle the deck each has chosen. The magician and spectator exchange decks. The magician takes the deck the spectator has chosen and shuffled; the spectator takes the magician's.

The magician instructs the spectator to cut the deck he is now holding. Likewise, the magician cuts the deck he now holds. Both privately memorize the card they've cut to. They each complete their cut, losing their card in the deck they are holding.

Once again the magician and spectator exchange decks. The spectator holds the magician's deck, containing the card the magician has chosen; the magician holds the spectator's deck, containing the card the spectator has chosen. Contrary to all expectation, the magician instructs the spectator to look for his secretly memorized card in the magician's deck as the magician looks for his own selected card within the spectator's deck.

Each removes his card from the deck he is holding and places it face-down on the table. The cards are turned over. Both cards are identical! Somehow, both the magician and spectator have miraculously cut to the same card.

SET-UP

No set-up is required.

METHOD

Present two normal decks. Instruct your spectator to select one of the decks. In our example, the spectator will choose the blue one. Allow the spectator to shuffle his deck. Simultaneously shuffle yours, the red deck. When you have finished, subtly take a peek at the bottom card, and remember it. Exchange decks with the spectator; he now has your deck and you have his. But the red deck, the deck the spectator now holds, has been secretly "marked" — you know what the bottom card is! This marker will allow you to locate the spectator's card, as you will see.

The spectator cuts his deck, and you cut yours. Instruct him to memorize the card he has cut to. Simultaneously, you cut your deck, and *pretend* to memorize the card you've cut to (**fig. 1**). Actually, the card you are looking at is disregarded; it has nothing to do with the trick. Instruct your spectator to place the card he has cut to onto the pile containing the top half of his deck. Have him place the bottom half of the deck on the top half of the deck, thereby completing the cut and losing his selected card in the center of his deck. Do as your spectator has just done. Complete your cut.

Once again, exchange decks. Instruct the spectator to look for the card that he cut to, to remove it from the blue deck he is now holding, and to place it face-down on the table. You, too, search for the card the spectator believes you've cut to, but what you're really looking for is that bottom card you peeked at, the marker. To actually find the spectator's card, hold your deck face-up in your left hand. Search the deck by pushing the cards, one at a time, into your right hand. The card you remove from the deck, the card the spectator has chosen, is the card *just before* the marker (**fig. 2**).

Place it face-down on the table. Turn over both cards, yours and the spectator's. It's a match.

PATTER

Express your conviction that you and your spectator have a lot more in common than is immediately evident. Tell him that you'd like to test these feelings with the help of a deck of cards. Ask for his permission. Go through all of the steps until you reach the point where both your card and the spectator's lie face-down on the table. Say, "You could have cut to any card; I could have cut to any card, but for some unknown reason... just coincidence...?" Turn over the cards. "We seem to have cut to the same card."

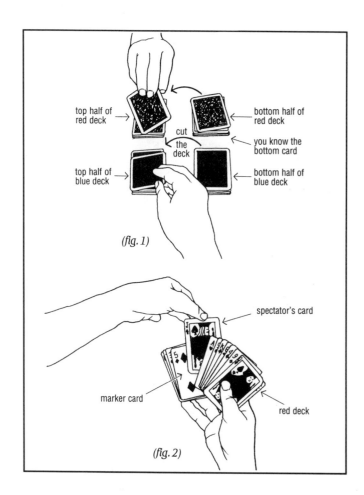

top half of red deck

bottom half of red deck

cut the deck

you know the bottom card

top half of blue deck

bottom half of blue deck

(fig. 1)

spectator's card

marker card

red deck

(fig. 2)

45

THREE DICE TRICK

A Stunt

Props
Three standard dice, one cup

EFFECT

The magician holds three dice, side by side, between his thumb and index finger, and positions them horizontally over the open mouth of a cup. The magician announces that he will allow only the middle die to fall down into the cup, while retaining the two outer dice between his fingertips. He explains that this is accomplished by opening and closing the thumb and index finger so very quickly and allowing the middle die to drop so rapidly, that the two outer dice remain stacked, side by side.

The magician challenges the spectator to attempt the task. But no matter how diligently the spectator tries, how rapidly his fingers spread apart and together, all three dice collapse in upon one another and fall down into the cup.

The magician is able to repeat the effect as many times as he likes.

SET-UP

None.

METHOD

The whole secret in performing this effect is to squeeze the two outer dice between your thumb and index finger as hard as you can. After exerting about four to five seconds' worth of pressure, the outer dice will stick to your fingers, giving you just enough time to quickly separate your thumb and index finger, to release the middle die **(fig. 1)**, and to bring the thumb and index finger back together with the two outer dice now side by side. You will still need to execute the move rather rapidly, but without squeezing the dice, the stunt is impossible to accomplish.

Of course, when your spectator attempts the task, he'll believe that it is speed alone, that is the key to the effect. His erroneous premise will bring him, repeatedly, to failure.

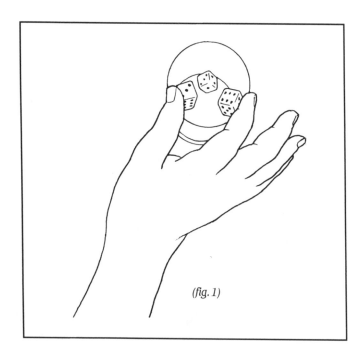

(fig. 1)

47

The Armchair Magician

Seven astounding effects made
possible by magic's second great principle

MISDIRECTION

THE SURPRISE VANISH

Category
Vanish

Props
One pen or pencil, and one coin

EFFECT

The magician borrows a coin. He places it in his left palm, shuts his fist, and declares that he will make the coin vanish. The magician takes a pencil and taps his closed fist with it three times. The magician opens his fist but the coin has not vanished. The magician explains that he will need to concentrate a little bit more and then he will attempt the vanish again. The magician pauses and then strikes his fist with the pencil three times. He opens his fist but the coin has still not disappeared. The magician says that he will try the stunt just one more time. The magician begins the sequence of three strikes but before he quite reaches the third strike he notices that his pencil is gone. Surprised, he exclaims, "I'm sorry, I was concentrating so hard that I made the pencil vanish instead."

SET-UP

None

METHOD

This effect works best if both you and the spectator are standing. It's also important to have your spectator as much to your left as possible. Your first two "failed" attempts at vanishing the coin are nothing more than a way to get your spectator accustomed to the way you strike your hand lightly with the pencil. The repetition

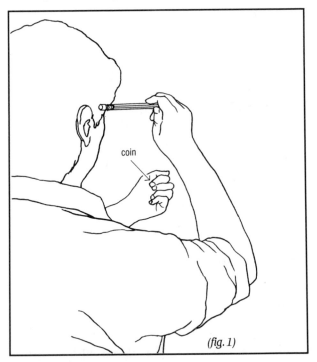

coin

(fig. 1)

creates a pattern that sets up your spectator's expectation of a specific routine.

With your spectator to your left, place the coin in your left hand. Hold the pen or pencil in your right hand. During the first attempt, take the pencil up to about eye level, coming down lightly three times in a row, counting aloud each strike. During your second attempt take the pencil a little bit higher and farther, this time up to the top of your right ear.

During your third and final attempt bring your pencil once again to ear level but this time after the count of two leave it up there, behind your ear **(fig. 1)**. It won't fall down. You can now see why it is important to have your spectator on your left side, not your right. Although your right hand is now empty, come down with it toward your shut fist as though you were still holding the pencil. Complete the count of three and act surprised at the sudden, unexpected disappearance of the pencil, apologizing profusely for your inappropriate and uncontained degree of concentration. You'll be surprised by how easy this effect is to perform, as well as by its strong impact.

THE CONJURER'S COIN TRICK

Category
Vanish

Prop
One quarter

EFFECT

The magician borrows a quarter. He claims that he can rub a coin
into his elbow, gradually dissolving it, until it completely vanishes.
The magician holds the coin to his elbow and rubs gently for
ten seconds. The magician removes his hand. The coin has vanished and is nowhere to be found. Both hands are shown empty.

SET-UP

This effect requires nothing except enthusiasm.

METHOD

Borrow a quarter from your spectator. (Any coin will
work, but the quarter is preferable because it is more visible than the smaller coins.) Take your left hand and place
it on the back of your neck; your elbow should now be
pointing out toward your spectator. Hold the quarter in
your right fingertips, pinching it with the thumb, the
pointer, and middle fingers. Start to rub the coin "into"
your elbow. Get ready now, here's the key move: After
you've rubbed for a few seconds, purposely drop the coin
onto the floor, but make it look entirely accidental. Say
something like "Oops" or "Sorry about that." As you bend
down to retrieve the coin, pick it up with your left hand
and pretend to place it back into your right. Act as
though the coin is now inside the right hand.
Immediately after pretending to transfer the coin from
the left to right hand, place your left hand at your neck,

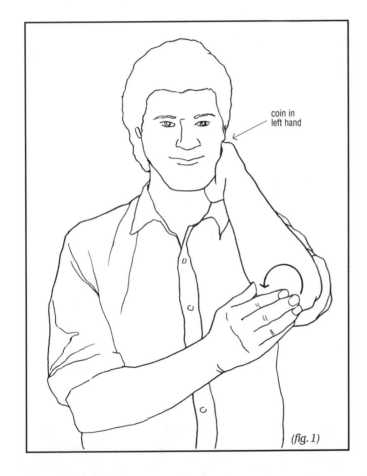

coin in left hand

(fig. 1)

and with your right hand begin to rub the "invisible" coin into your bent left elbow **(fig. 1)**.

You can do one of two things with the coin, which is actually hidden in your left hand. The safest maneuver is to open your left hand and drop the coin down your shirt collar. The other method is to lay it gently on the back of your neck; it will usually stay there.

To complete the effect, continue pretending to rub the coin into your elbow. Gradually remove your fingers from the elbow to reveal that the coin has mysteriously vanished, just as you said it would.

TIP

•We prefer disposing of the quarter hidden in the left hand by placing it on the neck. After showing your hands empty, you can retrieve the coin a minute or two later. You may even wish to experiment with unexpectedly producing it in some interesting way, like "pulling" it from someone's ear.

THE IMPOSSIBLE ROPES

Category
Transformation

Props
One 10 1/2" rope, one 24" rope, one 42" rope

EFFECT

The magician presents three ropes of different lengths, one very short rope, one very long rope, and one that's midway in size between the two. He holds one end of each rope, tip to tip. With his other hand he grasps the hanging bottom end of each rope and brings them up, one at a time, to meet the top ends; each rope has been folded in half, all six ends grasped in the magician's hand.

The magician takes three of the six ends in one hand and retains three in the other hand. He pulls in opposite directions. The ropes seem to stretch, until in place of the three unequal ropes there are now clearly three ropes, identical in size, stretched between the magician's hands. One hand releases its grip and the ropes hang freely.

As before, the magician folds the three ropes in half, holding all six ends tip to tip. He shakes his hand, allowing the ropes to unfold. Once again, three very different ropes hang freely from the magician's hand, one long, one medium, one short.

SET-UP

No set-up is required, no gimmicks are used. This classic miracle is performed from beginning to end, right under the nose of your spectator.

METHOD

Your left palm faces toward you, the thumb nearest to the ceiling. The back of the hand faces your spectator, and will be used later to conceal the secret positioning of the ropes. Grasp one end of each rope between the thumb and forefinger of the left hand. The ropes hang vertically, side by side, in the crook of your left hand, first the short rope (A), then the medium rope (B), then the longest rope (C). About 2" of each rope should extend visibly above the hand **(fig. 1)**. In this position, present the three ordinary ropes to your spectator. Demonstrate that there is nothing being concealed by transferring each rope, one at a time, from your left hand into your right, counting each rope as you do so.

Return the ropes to their original position in the left hand. Inform your spectator that you intend to fold each rope in half by bringing the bottom end of each rope up to meet its top end. Your key secret maneuver happens immediately: It is the way in which you will fold Rope A in half. No secret maneuvers will be used to fold Ropes B and C. With your right hand, take the bottom end of Rope A and fold it up so that it occupies the right-most position in your left hand. Now here's the move: Casually switch its position with the tip to its left, so that now the bottom end of Rope A is to the left of the top end of Rope C **(fig. 2)**.

The bottom end of Rope B is now folded up and placed all the way to the right of the other four pinched ends (to the right of the top end of Rope C).

The bottom end of Rope C is now folded up and placed all the way to the right of the other five pinched ends (to the right of the bottom end of Rope B).

All six ends of rope now extend upward from your left hand. The looped portions of Ropes B and C hang down visibly from your hand. Rope A's looped portion is concealed behind your hand; throughout the entire illusion, this small loop will remain hidden from view **(fig. 3)**.

You are now ready to "stretch" the ropes. With your right hand grasp the three right-most ends. With the left thumb and forefinger, retain your grasp on the remaining

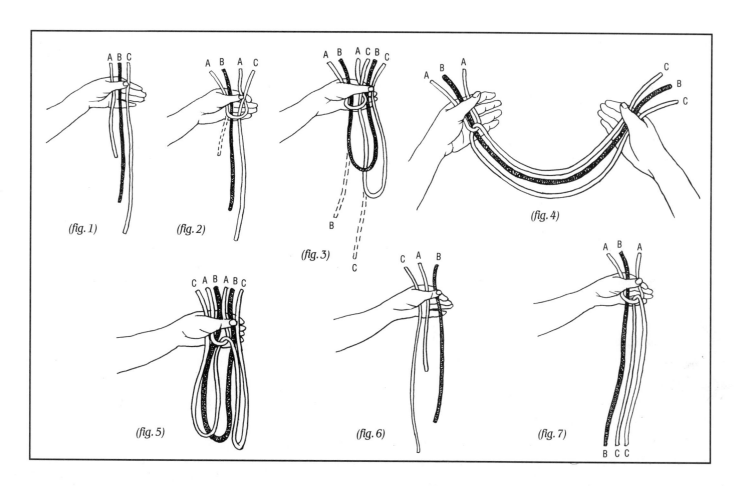

(fig. 1)

(fig. 2)

(fig. 3)

(fig. 4)

(fig. 5)

(fig. 6)

(fig. 7)

three ends. Pull the three right ends toward you as you pull the three left ends away. Pull slowly and smoothly; the ropes will appear to stretch. You are left holding three ends in your left hand and three in your right **(fig. 4)**. Let go of the three ends in your right hand. You now appear to be holding three equal ropes **(fig. 5)**.

To return the ropes to their former size, you will, once again, fold all three hanging ropes in half **(fig. 6)**. Before you begin this final sequence, casually arrange the ropes in your left hand so that the top end of Rope A is all the way to your left, the bottom end of Rope A is next to it, and the top end of Rope B is all the way to your right. Now bring the hanging end of the first strand all the way to your left (the top end of Rope C) up to the left-most position in your left hand (to the left of the top end of Rope A).

Bring the second hanging strand (the bottom of Rope C) up to the right-most position in your hand (to the right of the top end of Rope B).

The third hanging strand (the bottom of Rope B) must be placed so that it occupies the position third from the left (to the right of the top end of Rope A). Hold on to the three ropes to your left, let go of the three ropes to

your right. You'll be left holding one end of each original rope, one end of A, one end of B, one end of C **(fig. 7)**. The ropes appear to have suddenly returned to their unequal condition.

PATTER

The most popular patter associated with this effect involves variations on the metaphor of a dream. Here's one we enjoy using: "I had a dream I could change things, from chaos to order, from little to big. I dreamed I could make anyone a little more patient..." (Fold up Rope A.) "a little more compassionate..." (Fold up Rope B.) "a little less self-centered." (Fold up Rope C.) "I dreamed I could gather up all their traits, tip to tip, shake them up, pull them out, redistributed, reproportioned..." (Stretch the ropes.) "equal, balanced, whole." (Fold the ropes for your finale as you deliver the remaining patter.) "But you know how it is with dreams. You turn your head, the alarm goes off, and everything..." (Release the ropes.) "is exactly the way it was before."

CUT THE DECK

Category
Mentalism

Props
One deck of cards and one butter knife

EFFECT

Here's a quick and clever dinnertime effect. The spectator is asked to shuffle a deck of cards and then to place it face-down on the table. The magician announces that he will now cut the deck. He picks up a butter knife, and with a literal interpretation, slides the knife somewhere into the deck. Nobody, including the magician, can see the bottom card that was just cut to. The magician picks up the top half of the cut deck, still face-down, and holds it aside. The magician touches the knife to his forehead, saying that he can feel the energy of that bottom card. He announces the card he believes has been cut to. The top half of the deck is turned over. The intuitively perceived card is revealed.

SET-UP

Be sure to have access to a butter knife that is somewhat shiny and reflective; a tarnished one will be difficult to use. No further set-up is necessary.

METHOD

Ask the spectator to shuffle a deck of cards and to place them face-down on the table. Announcing that you will now cut the deck, pick up the butter knife. Approach the deck from its right side and slide the knife into it. Ask the spectator if he's satisfied, or if he wants you to slice elsewhere in the deck. Once agreed upon, pick up the top portion of the deck, the portion lying above the knife, about one quarter of an inch.

You'll find that the knife acts exactly like a mirror, clearly reflecting the card that is lying just above it **(fig. 1)**. Slide the knife, still in the deck, over to the lower left-hand corner of the cards. Pause for a second, just long enough to glimpse the reflection of the lower left-hand corner of the card that's been cut to. As you know, all cards in the face-down position will have their value notated in two places, in the top right-hand and bottom left-hand corners. (As an aside, "pip" cards are all cards that are numbered — for example, the Two of Diamonds or the Eight of Clubs. "Court" cards are the Jacks, Queens, and Kings.)

Remember, it will take you only a second to see the card's value, so try not to stare at the knife. Be subtle. At the moment you look into the knife, patter about your ability to pick up the energy and vibration of the card. Slide the knife out of the deck. Hold the top half of the face-down deck with your left hand, the knife with your

(fig. 1)

right. For effect, hold the knife to your forehead and pretend to concentrate. Pause. Announce the card you secretly saw.

TIPS

•Your goal when performing an effect involving mentalism is to make it appear to be an astonishing and authentic feat. The key is to act as though the task at hand is much harder than it actually is. Do not announce a chosen card too quickly — appear to be concentrating, even to look unsure of the image in your mind's eye. A nice, convincing touch is to state a particular card — a wrong card — and then to suddenly change your mind — now name the correct card.

•After a little bit of practice, you'll find that you don't need to lift the top portion of the deck very far at all in order to clearly and quite sufficiently see the card's reflection. In time you will also be able to take note of the reflection very rapidly and will not have to linger in this position. In any case, remember to distract your spectator's mind while noting the reflection. This is the whole essence of misdirection.

"I work alone, but I have an invisible
assistant — Miss Direction."
—*John Ramsey, sleight-of-hand artist*

"It's All Done With Mirrors...." The Hindu Rope Trick
The best known rope trick in the world may never have even existed, its mystery perpetuated by legends and lies.

Many claim to have seen the Hindu Rope Trick performed in India, but when questioned further they succumb, admitting that they themselves didn't actually see it, but they do know of someone, somewhere, who has.... First described in the 1300s, the trick begins when the magician tosses the end of a long, coiled rope up into the air. It rises to a great height and remains suspended. A young boy, the magician's assistant, climbs the rope to the top. The magician claps his hands. The boy vanishes, the rope collapses.

Whether or not it ever actually existed, the trick continues to be endlessly fascinating to both magicians and laymen. Howard Thurston (1869-1936) was one of many magicians who attempted to duplicate the effect. His methods included the use of invisible ropes, wires, and a rear projector. But he utilized the effect merely to draw people to the theater, quickly abandoning it because of its unreliability, its complete dependence on exact timing and synchronization of devices for it to work. The dramatic effect was, in fact, never again attempted by any well-known conjurer.

The best tricks, the most lasting, are those that depend primarily on the psychological principles of magic for their success. The devices are secondary; the devices support the principles, not vice versa.

ANYTHING CAN HAPPEN

Category
Penetration

Props
One salt shaker, one quarter, one table napkin

EFFECT

The magician and his spectator are sitting at a dinner table. The magician borrows a quarter, and placing it on the table in front of himself, announces that he will make the coin vanish. He picks up a salt shaker from the table and places it down on top of the coin. He explains that salt is quite magical, that it contains properties that wizards, throughout the ages, have employed. But, the magician continues to explain, these mystical properties can be awakened only in the dark; he proceeds to cover the coin and salt shaker with a dinner napkin. The magician snaps his fingers and then lifts up the shaker with the napkin, but the coin has not vanished.

The magician exclaims, "Oh, I forgot to say the magic words, 'salt and pepper, sugar and spice, coin please vanish, coin be nice.'" (We don't really expect you to say this, we're just being frivolous; create a phrase that suits your own personality and style.) The magician replaces the napkin and salt shaker on top of the coin, says his magic words, snaps his fingers, removes the napkin and shaker, but again, the coin has not vanished.

"I've made yet another mistake," he apologizes. "I've said the wrong magic words. Those were the words that make the salt shaker vanish!" The magician places his hand above the salt shaker and napkin and slaps the napkin down on the table, flattening it; the salt shaker has vanished! The magician explains to his spectator that the salt shaker didn't actually disappear, but that it has merely penetrated through the table. The magician reaches under the table and comes up with the shaker. The spectator says, "That's the most amazing thing I've ever seen. Can you do something with the gravy?" The magician says, "It probably just needs a little salt."

SET-UP

None.

METHOD

This is a classic piece of impromptu magic; there is absolutely no set-up, and it can be done at any dinner table, anytime, anywhere. Once again, we'll be employing the technique of "lapping" (see 'Coin Through Table'). Place the coin on the table, and cover the salt shaker with a napkin. Through the draped napkin grab the salt shaker at its base, and place them both over the coin. Be sure to keep the napkin tightly wrapped around the shaker.

Make your magic gesture, say your words, and lift up both the cloth and shaker together. Do not remove the cloth from the shaker. Act surprised; the coin has not vanished. Now you are ready to secretly "lap" the salt shaker. As you lift the napkin and shaker, bring them right to the edge of the table, just over your lap. Loosen your grip ever so slightly, just enough to allow the salt shaker to drop down onto your lap from under the napkin **(fig.1)**. The napkin will retain the exact shape of the salt shaker; to the spectator, it will look as though it is still under the napkin.

Gently place the empty mold of the napkin over the coin. Of course, don't let go. With your other hand, make a magic gesture or say your magic words. Slap the napkin straight down to the table, flattening it. It will look as though the salt shaker vanished at that very instant.

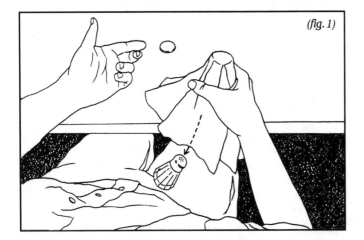

(fig. 1)

Reach under the table and retrieve the shaker from your lap, but before revealing it to your spectator, continue, for a few seconds, to look as though you are reaching far under the table; you don't want your spectator to think it was sitting hidden on your lap, all along. Bring out the salt shaker that appears to have miraculously penetrated the table.

TIPS

•When you "fail" to vanish the coin, it's very important to act surprised. You might want to go as far as turning the coin over, as though examining it and searching for a reason for your failure. During all that activity, it becomes very easy to draw back your hand with the shaker and to let it drop down onto your lap, virtually unobserved. As long as you keep your attention and your eyes on the coin, the spectator will neither see nor remember your other action.

•This trick also works well with almost any type of drinking glass. In place of a table napkin, you'll find that paper towels and sheets of paper are also very effective. Paper molds itself extremely well to the shape of small objects.

NEEDLES IN A HAYSTACK

Category
Revelation

Prop
One deck of cards

EFFECT

At first glance, this trick appears to be rather lengthy and complex, but *please* read it through, try it and learn it. It's actually very simple to do and is one of those effects that seems to be nothing short of a miracle. We promise you that your audience will be talking about it long after you've taken your leave. This trick is truly a reputation-maker; at least it has been for us....

The magician presents a deck of cards and asks a spectator to thoroughly shuffle it. The spectator is then instructed to cut the deck into four piles, as equal as possible. The spectator is asked to select one of the four piles, pick it up, and to count, to himself, the number of cards in his chosen pile. The magician tells the spectator that the number must be a two-digit number, i.e., greater than nine, and if it is not, he must add to his pile as many as he needs to fit the requirement.

The spectator is instructed to silently add the two digits together, to take that final number, and to count down that number of cards from the top of his pile. The spectator looks at the card he has counted down to and memorizes it. The spectator is told to square his pile, with his memorized card buried within it, and to place the pile face-down in front of himself on the table. During this entire sequence, the magician has his back turned to the spectator so that all information about the position of the chosen card is completely hidden from him.

A second spectator is now asked to choose one pile from among the remaining three and to repeat the sequence of steps taken by the first spectator.

The magician, once again, faces his spectators, lifts up the two piles that were not selected, and places one of those piles on top of the first spectator's deck and places the other pile on top of the second spectator's deck.

There are now two piles sitting face-down on the table. Either one of the spectators is asked to select one of the two piles and to turn it face-up. The magician shuffles the selected face-up pile together with the remaining face-down pile; he now holds a pile that contains both face-up and face-down cards, randomly mixed together.

He squares the pile and does a hand spread, revealing to his spectators that the cards have, in fact, been mixed.

The magician silently scans through the pile a few times and finally announces that he believes he's found the two secretly memorized cards. The magician places the pile in his right hand and tosses it into his left. Two cards, and only two, remain behind in his right hand. The magician turns them both face-up. They are the two selected cards.

SET-UP

None.

METHOD

As we've said, it sounds rather lengthy, but as you run through the steps you'll see that the entire effect is really quite easy to execute and is nothing short of miraculous. Here we go....

Begin by presenting a full deck of cards. Ask your spectator to shuffle the deck as much as he'd like and then to cut the deck into four relatively equal piles. If the four piles seem to be very unequal, ask your spectator to adjust them; it's very important that the piles are as equal as possible. Ask him to select one of the four piles and, as we've previously described, have him count the cards in his selected pile **(fig. 1)**. If the pile contains fewer than ten cards, instruct him to remove a few cards from another pile and to add them to his selected pile. The total number of cards must be a two-digit number. Let's assume his pile contains fifteen cards. He would add together the numbers one and five, which yield the number six. He would therefore count down six cards from the top of his pile, would memorize this sixth card, leave it where it is in his pile, square the cards, and place the pile face-down on the table in front of himself. It's certainly acceptable to use an example like this one when explaining to your spectator what you expect him to do.

A second spectator is now chosen to participate. He is instructed to follow exactly the same sequence of steps as your first spectator. He chooses a pile from among the three remaining piles and proceeds from there, culminating in the selection of a card. The second spectator's pile is then placed face-down on the table. You may turn your back to your spectators as they count their piles and find their cards, emphasizing the total secrecy of their choices.

Two unused piles of cards remain on the table. Take one of these face-down piles and place it on top of the first spectator's pile. Take the other pile and place it on top of the second spectator's pile **(fig. 2)**.

Ask either one of your spectators to select one of the two piles that are now lying on the table and to turn it face-up. Thoroughly mix together the pile of face-up cards with the pile of face-down cards **(fig. 3)**. You may do a quick hand spread to demonstrate to your spectators that the two piles have been truly mixed; some cards are face-up and some are face-down. So far, everything you've done is exactly as was described under "Effect."

Now you're ready to find the secretly selected cards. Pick up the shuffled pile and hold it in your left hand; it does not matter which way you hold it, top card up or bottom card up. Count, to yourself, the first ten face-up cards. Do not include in your count any of the face-down cards! Even if there are five or six face-down cards in a row, do not count them. On your way to the tenth face-up card, push each and every card that you pass, the face-up ones along with the face-down ones, into your right hand. Each succesive card goes beneath the previous one so that the order is not changed. When you get to the tenth face-up card, you will have a small pile in your right hand. Turn that pile over on top of the pile remaining in your left hand. That tenth card, as unlikely as it sounds, will always be one of the chosen cards. This chosen card is, therefore, now sitting face-down on top of your pile.

Now take this entire pile in your left hand and turn it over so that the bottom card is now the top one. You are ready to find the second selected card. As before, count the first ten face-up cards, remembering not to include in your count any of the face-down cards that you pass on your way. The cards are pushed, as before, from your left hand into your right. When you reach the tenth face-up card, turn the pile in your right hand over on top of the pile in your left. You have just found the second card; it now sits on top of the pile in your left hand! One of the

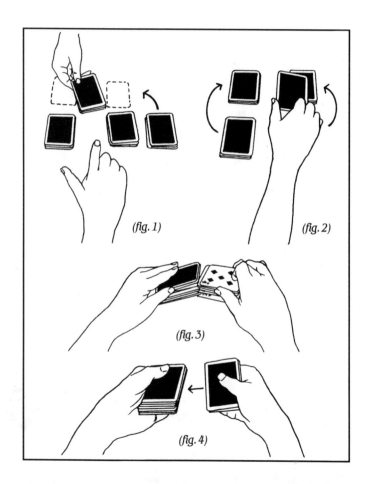

(fig. 1)

(fig. 2)

(fig. 3)

(fig. 4)

two selected cards is on top of your deck, the other is on the bottom.

Put the entire pile into your right hand. Place your right thumb on top of the pile, your pointer and middle finger beneath it. You are now holding the pile with only three fingers, one on top, two on the bottom. This final move is extremely dramatic, and with very little practice, can be easily executed. If you toss the deck into your left hand by giving your wrist a short, sharp flick, the entire pile will slip out from between the top card and bottom card; the two secretly selected cards remain behind in your right hand **(fig. 4)**. It's very much like ripping away a tablecloth and leaving the intact dishes behind on the bare table. Keep your hands close together, only inches apart from each other; you're not trying to impress your audience with how far you can throw a deck and catch it! If your hands are too far apart, the cards will drop before reaching their destination.

The idea is to make it appear as though the two cards could be coming from anywhere inside the deck. With a little practice you'll find that the illusion is simple to achieve.

This trick is based on an ingenious mathematical principle. We, unfortunately, do not know anything about the inventor of the effect, but we're happily indebted.

TIPS

• Please be aware that you must use a full deck of fifty-two cards. The trick does not work with fifty-one cards, and it does not work if the Jokers are not removed! This effect is based on exact principles of mathematics.

• As described, we recommend doing this trick with two spectators instead of only one. The effect is quite involved, and we find that one spectator has difficulty remembering two cards. But if you must use only one spectator, you might suggest to him that he write down his two selected cards so as not to risk forgetting them.

• Work on your presentation. When you search for the two cards, act as though you are concentrating. Make the task appear to be harder and more mysterious than it actually is, and you'll be well on your way to making a name for yourself....

ROBERT-HOUDIN (1805-1871)

Robert-Houdin, born Jean-Eugene Robert, was the son of a watchmaker in Blois, France. At eighteen, Robert-Houdin embarked upon the study of law, but his mechanical interests led him back to his father's trade. According to his autobiography, a simple incident changed the entire course of his life. While looking for a book on watchmaking in a shop in Blois, he was, by mistake, given several volumes of an old encyclopedia, one of which contained an exposition of magic called "Scientific Amusements." Robert-Houdin turned his full attention to magic.

Robert-Houdin was a prolific inventor, applying his skill at clock repairing and building to the craft of stage illusion. He opened his own theater in 1845, and retired from performing in 1854. In 1856, he came out of retirement when the French government called upon him to help stop an uprising in Algeria. Robert-Houdin's task was to intimidate the rebels by exhibiting his sleight-of-hand tricks, which were far superior to the work of the Arab magicians or marabouts, whose influence was usually held responsible for the revolts.

Robert-Houdin spent the remainder of his life devoted to his inventions and writings.

Category
Transposition

Props
One drinking glass filled with water, one coin,
one handkerchief

EFFECT

The magician covers a filled water glass with a handkerchief or napkin. He removes a coin from his pocket, places it into his left hand, closes his fist and suspends it over the covered mouth of the glass. The magician opens his fist, but the coin has vanished. The spectator is immediately instructed to remove the handkerchief and to look down into the glass. The spectator peers down into the glass of water and there he sees the coin sitting on the bottom of the glass. The magician picks the glass of water up off the table, and there is the coin, now sitting beneath the glass, on the table. The coin has not only invisibly dropped from his hand through the handkerchief and into the water, but has penetrated right through the bottom of the glass to the table!

SET-UP

When you are alone, place a filled glass of water right on top of a coin (**fig. 1**). This is a fascinating illusion; the coin can be seen only when looking directly down into the glass. Take a step or two away from the table. You'll see that the coin is no longer visible! Experimenting with this illusion, on your own, will also give you a rather precise idea of how close to the table you may allow your spectator to stand. You will not need to keep him very far away, but bear in mind, not too close either. You be the judge.

METHOD

Invite your spectator to step over to the table, and tell him you are going to show him something very interesting. Take a handkerchief and place it over your prepared glass filled with water. In front of your spectator, remove a coin from your pocket. Place the coin on the pinky and ring finger of your palm-up right hand; place it just at the point where the two fingers are joined to the palm of the hand **(fig. 2)**. You'll find that if you now slightly curl your fingers, you can turn your hand over, and the coin will stay in place. Concealing a small object in an apparently open hand is called "palming"; this particular version is called a "finger-palm." Palming is a very useful

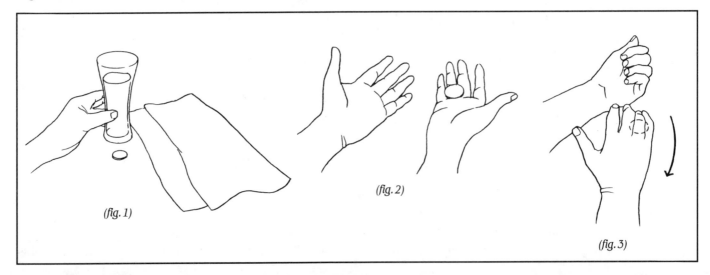

(fig. 1)

(fig. 2)

(fig. 3)

skill to acquire in your study of magic. Practice it over and over until it becomes easy, which it will.

Let's take it from the top. Once the coin is sitting in the correct place on your palm-up right hand, pretend to transfer the coin into your left hand by turning the "open" right palm over, just above your open left palm. Close your left fist, as if grasping the invisible coin, and allow the right hand with the concealed coin to just drop to your lap or side **(fig. 3)**.

Open your left palm, revealing that the coin has vanished. Within an instant, instruct your spectator to approach the table, to look over the glass and to remove the handkerchief. Utilize these few seconds of misdirection to dispose of the palmed coin in your right hand. As the spectator looks down into the glass, he will now, for the first time, see the coin that you secretly placed beneath it. It appears to him as though the coin is sitting in the water, on the bottom of the glass.

Instruct your spectator to lift up the glass, revealing that the coin has not only passed silently and invisibly from your hand through the handkerchief and into the water, but has penetrated right through the glass bottom to the table.

TIPS

•The finger-palm is easy to learn, and if you're a good actor, can be extremely deceptive. Just execute the move casually, and remember, you do not need to curl your fingers very much; the natural curve of the fingers is sufficient.

•After palming the coin and pretending to transfer it to your left fist, *immediately* instruct your spectator to approach the table, to remove the handkerchief, and to look down into the glass. If you vanish the coin and then pause, for even a few seconds, your spectator is given time to think. His mind is afforded the opportunity to formulate undesirable questions, questions like,"Where did the coin go?" And it's a sure bet that he'll then pronounce those famous words,"Show me your other hand!" Do not give your spectator that time; the moment you open your left fist, begin to draw him into your next set of instructions. Go so far as to physically place your hand on him and to pull him gently to the table and glass.

The

ARMCHAIR MAGICIAN

Eight belief-defying tricks that
capitalize on the third key magic principle

CONCEALMENT

THE REAPPEARING MATCH

Category
Restoration

Prop
One book of matches, preferably not full

EFFECT

The magician slowly and deliberately counts the matches in a book of matches. He and the spectator are both in agreement as to how many matches there are. A match is randomly pulled from the book and lit by the magician. The match is blown out and discarded. The magician taps the closed matchbook, and when it is reopened we see, along with the other unused matches, the burned and discarded match still firmly attached to the book. The original total number of matches has not altered.

SET-UP

Prior to presentation, remove one match from the book. Next, bend, one of the matches in the front row of the book, out and down, but do not detach it. Close the cover, leaving the bent-down match exposed. Strike the loose match and use it to light the match you've bent out. Blow out both matches. Discard the detached match,

as it has nothing to do with the effect that follows. Now hold the matchbook in your left hand. Conceal the bent-out match with the burned head beneath your left thumb (**fig. 1**). You are now ready to present the effect.

METHOD

Holding your prepared book of matches with your left hand, count together with your spectator the number of exposed matches. (In our example there are ten.) With your right hand, tear out a match from the front row of the book. Without moving your left thumb from its original position, strike and light the detached match. Move your hands apart so that the book is somewhat off to your left, the lit match off to your right. Ask the spectator to blow out the match whenever he chooses to. During this moment of distraction (misdirection), take the opportunity to quickly use your left thumb to fold the concealed burned match back up into the book and then to close the cover with your left hand. Visibly discard the detached match.

Tap the closed matchbook or use any magical gesture you please. Reopen the book and indicate to the spectator that the apparently discarded burned match is still firmly attached to the book. Together count the total number of matches. (In our example, there would be ten, one burned and nine unused.)

TIPS

•Using a full book of matches will slow down the pace of this trick. We recommend using a book that has no

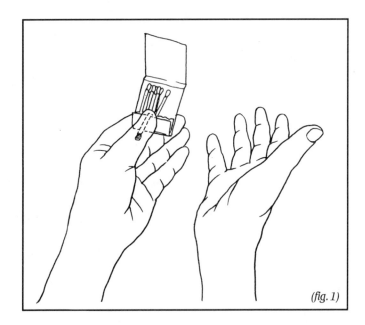

(fig. 1)

more than twelve matches remaining.

•When discarding the match that the spectator has blown out, allow it to cool and then place it into your pocket. Do not put it into the ashtray or anywhere on the table. This match should not remain in sight or else the overall effect will be diminished.

PATTER

A) *Straightforward:*

Straight explanation works perfectly well with this illusion. Explain what you appear to be doing as you do it.

B) *Metaphor:*

As you open the matchbook with the concealed burned match, say, "Perhaps you have the same experience I do: Things come back to haunt me, things I think are over and gone, something I've said, someone I've known, a bad habit … a book of matches. Count them. I remove one, light it, blow it out." Close the book and throw the detached match away. "Out of sight, out of mind? Do you have the same experience I do? Things I think are over and gone are just around the corner, waiting."

Point to the burned match still attached, and count them all.

HARRY KELLAR (1849-1922)
Born in Erie, Pennsylvania, Kellar became a solo performer at the age of sixteen. Within a decade he was touring with his own show, which was made up entirely of large-scale illusions; his levitation of Princess Kar nac became an especially famous component.

Kellar's trademark was the little red devils that populated all his posters. Said Kellar of the devils and the unbridled power of imagination, "The people who came to the show expecting to see devils generally did see them, or thought they did — all over the stage and even into the theater lobby, on the way out." Kellar retired in 1908, officially naming Howard Thurston as his successor.

*"To know a trick is nothing. To do it is something. To present it is **all**."*
—Silvan, Italy's premier magician

THE MYSTICAL SILK

Category
Production and Vanish

Props
*One piece of colored silk, approximately nine inches square,
and one thumb tip*

EFFECT

The magician shows his spectator that both of his hands are completely empty. With one hand he makes a fist. He reaches into his empty fist and begins to pull out a piece of silk, which has suddenly materialized. He stuffs the silk back into his fist. He opens both hands. The silk has vanished. His hands are empty.

SET-UP

Conceal the silk inside the thumb tip and place the tip on your right thumb. It is best to leave about one inch of fabric remaining outside the tip before putting your thumb into the tip. The silk will wrap around your thumb, making the fit more snug. Of course, before beginning your presentation, make sure the silk is entirely hidden inside the tip.

METHOD

Stand directly in front of your spectator. Show him that your hands are empty. Do not say, "Look, my hands are empty." The mere suggestion of emptiness will arouse suspicion. To reveal your empty hands, and to assure that the tip will not be seen, relax your fingertips, face your palms out toward your audience, and point the tips of your thumbs directly at them, parallel to the floor. The spectator will see only the tips of your thumbs and will observe nothing out of the ordinary **(fig. 1)**.

Make a loose fist with your left hand. Using the thumb and pointer of your right hand, reach into your left fist. Before withdrawing your fingers, leave the thumb tip behind, hidden by the fingers of your left fist **(fig. 2)**. Do not hold your fist below eye level. We do not want our spectators to be able to look down into it and see the thumb tip. With your right thumb and pointer, pull the silk slowly out of your left fist, but do not pull it out completely. Leave part of it remaining in the tip **(fig. 3)**.

With alternating fingers, push the silk completely back into the hidden tip. When it's the thumb's turn to push, push the thumb forcefully enough into the tip so that when you remove your thumb from the fist, the tip will come along with it. Even after you've made this move, use your other fingers to continue pretending to push the silk more compactly into your fist. Keep your eyes on the empty left fist, the fist where the silk is assumed to be. Flash your "empty" right hand with the hidden silk and

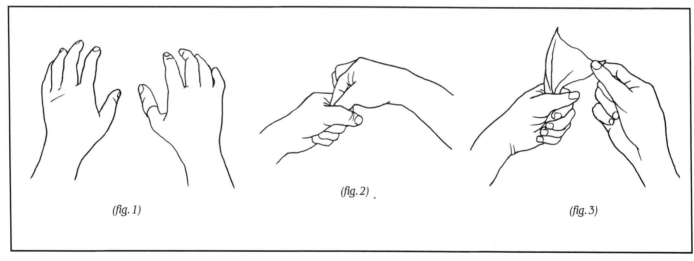

(fig. 1)

(fig. 2) .

(fig. 3)

tip, but pay no attention to this hand. Reach into your right pocket for magic dust, or a wand, or anything you wish. As you do this, leave the thumb tip behind. Sprinkle the magic dust on your left hand. Open your left hand and show your spectators that it is completely empty.

TIPS

• There is no need to angle the tip in an attempt to hide it. While performing with a thumb tip, move naturally. Do not look at it, disregard it completely. Act as if you are not even wearing one. As with anything new, this may at first be difficult to do but with a little practice it will be easily accomplished.

• Because of the surprising invisibility of the thumb tip, do not be concerned if you are unable to discard it immediately upon completion of the effect. You can unobtrusively get rid of it when you reach into your bag or pocket for the next prop in your routine.

PATTER

A) Straightforward:

You begin your patter for "The Mystical Silk" even before your spectators fully realize that you've begun to perform a trick. As you show your hands are empty and begin to make a fist and secretly deposit the tip, say, "Watch closely. Don't blink. Magic happens very quickly." Before they have time to think, you've produced a silk. As you push the silk back into the hidden tip, advise them of your intent to vanish it. As you reinsert your right thumb into the tip, ask your spectators to count with you, "one, two, three." Before they quite reach "three" reveal that the silk has vanished. "Magic happens quickly," you say.

B) Metaphor:

Showing your hands are empty, say, "You know how it is with life: easy come, easy go." Continue to speak your patter as you make your fist, deposit the tip, and produce the silk. "Suddenly, without warning, you have something you never before had. Something you've always wanted. You hold it, see it, feel it. It's real. And then, without warning…" Reinsert the thumb, deposit the silk, and vanish it while you continue to speak. "We blink our eyes, count to three, one, two…" Show your empty hands. "And it's gone. Gone, as if it were never even here."

BEAD PENETRATION

Category
Penetration

Props
*One wooden bead with a hole drilled through its center,
two shoelaces*

EFFECT

The magician presents a small wooden bead that has
a small hole drilled through the center. Two shoelaces have
been threaded through the bead. The bead is placed in the
spectator's palm. The spectator is asked to close his fist
around the bead, allowing the four loose shoelace ends to
hang freely from his fist. The magician takes hold of two
ends, one on each side, and ties a single knot around the top
of the spectator's fist. The magician now grabs all four ends
with both hands and proceeds to pull the two shoelaces in
opposite directions. The two laces appear to penetrate both
the bead and the spectator's hand, leaving the bead behind
in the spectator's tight fist and the magician holding on to
the two intact, quite ordinary laces.

SET-UP

This set-up entails threading the two shoelaces through the bead in a special, concealed manner, prior to presentation. When you are done it will appear as though two shoelaces have been quite normally threaded through a hole in a bead.

Take one shoelace and double it, end to end. Take the resulting loop and push it through the hole in the bead until a small portion of the loop emerges from the other side. Now take the second shoelace and double it, creating a loop. Take this second loop and thread it right through the first loop **(fig.1)**. Take the loose ends of the first lace and pull on them gently until both loops are hidden inside the bead. Four ends of shoelace now hang loosely, making it appear as though the two shoelaces are running straight through the bead **(fig. 2)**.

METHOD

Introduce the wooden bead with the two laces threaded through it. Place the threaded bead on the spectator's palm. The four loose ends hang down over his palm, two on each side. Ask the spectator to tightly close his fist and turn his hand palm-side down. Take any two opposite ends and tie a single knot around the top of his hand **(fig. 3)**. Take the two hanging left ends in one hand and the two right ends in the other. Pull **(fig. 4)**. The laces will release from the bead and the fist, leaving the bead behind in the spectator's hand and you holding on to the two intact shoelaces **(fig. 5)**.

TIP

•Never hold the two shoelaces without also holding on to the bead, as this would appear unnatural to the unsuspecting spectator. If it were indeed threaded normally, the bead would be free to slide up and down the laces. In this prepared threading the bead cannot move but will hang suspended in place.

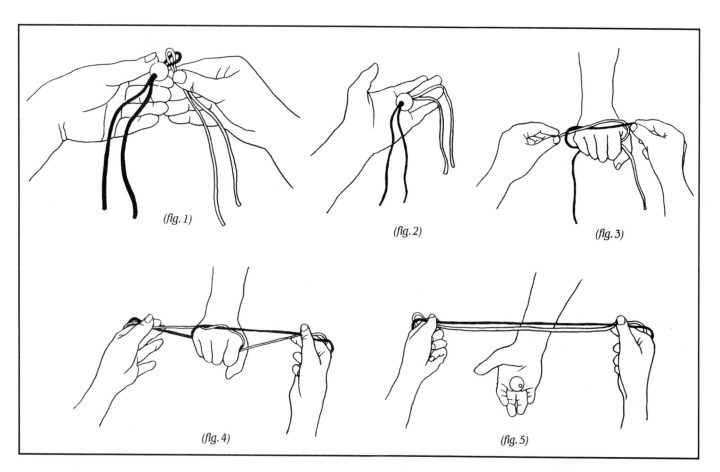

(fig. 1)

(fig. 2)

(fig. 3)

(fig. 4)

(fig. 5)

THE FLYING CARDS

Category
Transposition

Props
Two legal-size envelopes and one deck of cards

EFFECT

The magician holds an ordinary deck of cards and begins to deal them face-down on the table. The spectator, whenever he chooses, stops the magician and together they count the total number of cards dealt. The magician presents the spectator with two envelopes. The spectator is asked to examine both of them and to select one. The other is discarded. The magician scoops up the pile of dealt cards and places them into the chosen envelope. The envelope is sealed and handed to the spectator to hold.

The magician picks up the remaining portion of the deck and claims that he will make four cards fly out of the deck he is holding and into the spectator's sealed envelope. The spectator rips open his envelope and counts the cards inside. Four additional cards have indeed made their way into his sealed and secure envelope.

SET-UP

Take any four cards from the deck and hide them neatly underneath the two stacked envelopes. Place the pile off to your right on the table. When you begin your presentation, the spectator will see only two ordinary envelopes lying haphazardly, one on top of the other.

METHOD

Hold the deck face-down in your right hand. Begin the effect by silently dealing a few cards, about three or four, down onto the table. Allow them to fall into a somewhat sloppy pile. At that point, as you continue to slowly deal, ask your spectator to stop you whenever he chooses **(fig. 1)**. It doesn't matter what point he stops you at; it is irrelevant. In our example we will pretend that twelve cards have been dealt. Put down the unused portion of the deck and set it aside. Pick up the dealt cards and slowly and deliberately count them aloud. The next step is crucial.

With your right hand pick up the two envelopes along with the four cards still hidden beneath. Toss the two envelopes and the four cards onto the pile of twelve dealt cards. You have just secretly added the four extra cards

to the previously counted pile. This is why it was important for you to deal a few cards before allowing the spectator to stop you. Had he stopped you after having dealt only two or three cards there would have been no way for you to add the four additional cards without him seeing the obvious increase in the size of the pile.

Now ask the spectator to carefully inspect both envelopes and to choose one of them. Discard the other. Pick up the pile of sixteen cards and place them into the

(fig. 1)

selected envelope. Remember, the spectator believes that the original pile of twelve is what's going into the envelope. Seal the envelope and hand it to the spectator to hold.

Pick up the unused portion of the deck and claim that you will make four cards invisibly fly from the deck into the spectator's envelope. At this point, before revealing the culmination of the effect, it adds an interesting touch to make a magical gesture — wave your hand over the deck or riffle through it four times. Place the deck on the table. Tell the spectator to rip open his sealed envelope. Allow the spectator to count the cards he finds inside. There are now sixteen.

TIPS

• When you deal the cards, it's important to allow them to fall into a slightly sloppy pile on the tabletop. If the pile is too neat, the addition of the four cards becomes more easily detectable.

• It may be tempting to use one envelope instead of two, but be forewarned: using two gives you a logical reason to lift them up and toss them down in front of the spectator. One envelope would more logically be handed directly to him, short-circuiting the crucial move.

"THINKING ON YOUR FEET..."
HARRY BLACKSTONE, SR.
(1885-1965)

While on a world tour, Harry Blackstone performed for an expectant South American audience. But, unfortunately for the magician, the South Americans were witnessing tricks that they'd seen their own witch doctors perform, and despite the magician's considerable reputation and fame they remained completely unimpressed. Mr. Blackstone, responsive to the moment and thinking on his feet, stopped his prepared routine midstream, reached into his mouth, and proceeded to pull out his dentures. The crowd went wild. They had never, ever before seen a man pull all the teeth out of his mouth and then put them all back. This even their witch doctors could not do. Harry Blackstone returned home, his reputation undiminished.

84

THE VANISHING LIT CIGARETTE

Category
Vanish

Props
*One thumb tip, one lit cigarette (burned halfway down),
and one handkerchief*

EFFECT

The magician borrows a handkerchief from a spectator and drapes
it over his fist. He creates a well by poking some of the fabric down
into his fist. The magician borrows a lit cigarette and places the lit
end into the handkerchief. The magician slowly lifts the handkerchief off his fist. The lit cigarette has completely vanished, the fabric has not been harmed.

SET-UP

Place the empty thumb tip on your right thumb.

METHOD

Borrow a handkerchief from a spectator. If none is
offered, use a cloth table napkin or borrow any item that
can be draped over your fist. Drape it over your left fist.
With the middle finger of your right hand, create a well by
poking some of the fabric down into your fist. To create

this well, you will first use your middle finger, then your
pointer, then your thumb. Secretly leave the thumb tip
behind in your left fist, keeping your fist at eye level so
that the tip remains concealed.

Borrow a lit cigarette. Place the lit end into the thumb
tip (**fig. 1**). Using your right thumb and pointer, begin to
twist and put the cigarette out. When you are confident
that it has been extinguished and will not burn you, use
your right thumb to completely crush the cigarette,

enabling you to slip the tip back onto your right thumb **(fig. 2)**.

With your right thumb and pointer grab any corner of the fabric, slowly lifting it up off your fist. Reveal that the cigarette has vanished and that the handkerchief has not been burned. If the handkerchief you used is your own, you can secretly dispose of the thumb tip while placing the handkerchief back into your pocket.

TIPS

• The cigarette will not burn through the thumb tip, but as a precaution, you can place a small piece of tinfoil inside the tip. If you do not use the foil and the tip becomes blackened inside, the tip can be cleaned with alcohol and a cotton swab.

• Use your own handkerchief only as a last resort. This trick will have a far more dramatic effect if you use a borrowed item. Borrow a sweater, a necktie, anything at all that is large enough to be draped over your fist.

PATTER

A) Straightforward:

While draping the fabric over your fist, say, "I'd like to

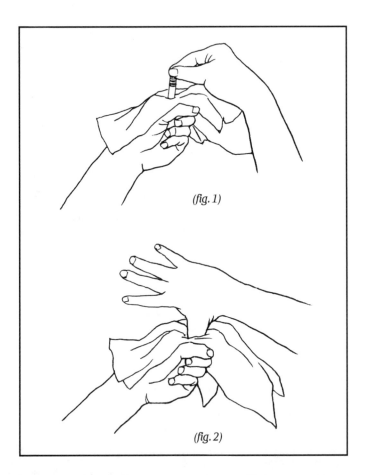

(fig. 1)

(fig. 2)

try something I've been working on. I hope it works." As you drop the lit cigarette into the well, explain your actions and intentions. "I will drop a cigarette into the fabric, burn a hole, and then restore the fabric to its original condition." Address the spectator's concern by saying, "No kidding, I've done this before." As you crush and extinguish the cigarette, add suspense and humor by asking, "Was this (item) expensive?" Whatever the answer, say, "Good, because the garment is unharmed…." Show the fabric with the hole restored. Now reveal your surprise ending. "And the cigarette has vanished."

B) Story:

Declare that you've discovered a surefire way to make anyone give up smoking. Express that though many methods are used, few succeed. Accept the challenge of a volunteer and borrow an item belonging to him. Make your fist, drape the fabric, deposit the tip, take his cigarette. As you place the lit cigarette into the fabric, tell him your intent is to burn a hole in this item so that he will always remember the moment he quit. Ask him if the item was precious. "It doesn't matter," you tell him, "because the garment is unharmed but the cigarette is gone."

"PLAY IT UP BIG"
HARRY HOUDINI (1874-1926)

Harry Houdini's name became a household word even before the days of television. Although his performances are not preserved on film, it is said that Houdini's name is mentioned somewhere in the world every twenty minutes. Yes, he was an extraordinary escape artist, but it was his genius as a showman, his sense of the dramatic, and his understanding of how to apply it that truly accounts for his fame.

Harry Houdini comes onstage. Manacled, tied, he is locked in a packing case. The curtain is drawn and the audience waits. Houdini rather quickly escapes from his restraints, but he does not emerge from the curtain just yet. He slips backstage, eats lunch, reads his paper. Thirty minutes later, just at the point when he knows his audience, mad with anticipation, can't stand to wait even a second longer, he bursts through the curtain, freed, out of breath, his hair a mess. Houdini believed that if he emerged too quickly people would think it was all too easy.

WATER SUSPENSION

Category
Levitation

Props
One thumb tip, one dollar bill, a small piece of paper,
one shot glass filled with water

EFFECT

The magician borrows a dollar bill, any denomination, and rolls it into the shape of a tube. He then takes a small piece of paper, crumples it into a ball, and stuffs it into the bottom end of the vertically held rolled bill; he tells the spectator that the crumpled paper will act like a bottle cork. The magician lifts the shot glass filled with water and pours the liquid into the top end of the tube. He explains that, impossible as it sounds, it is the paper cork that is keeping the water from pouring out.

The magician then removes the ball of paper, but the water still does not pour out from the dollar bill tube; it remains magically suspended. He replaces the cork and pours the water out of the bill and back into the shot glass. The magician unrolls the borrowed bill and returns it to the spectator for examination.

SET-UP

Prior to presentation, place the thumb tip on your right thumb.

METHOD

Borrow a bill of any denomination. Hold the bill up to your spectators, demonstrating that it is ordinary and not being tampered with in any way. Roll the bill around the thumb tip on your right thumb. After you've gone around one complete time, remove your thumb from the bill, leaving the tip behind, concealed by the bill **(fig. 1)**. Continue to roll the bill around the thumb tip, forming a tube. Hold it vertically, so that the openings are at the top and bottom. Take a small piece of paper and crumple it into a ball. Lightly tuck it into the bottom of your tube. Explain that the paper will act like a bottle cork.

Pick up the shot glass and pour the water into the rolled bill; it is, of course, actually being poured into the concealed thumb tip **(fig. 2)**. Remove the paper cork and claim that without the aid of the cork, you are now magically suspending the water. Replace the cork and pour the water from the "bill" back into the shot glass.

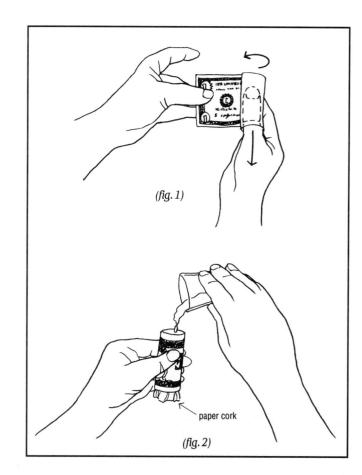

(fig. 1)

paper cork

(fig. 2)

Remove the cork.

Reinsert your right thumb into the tip, which is still inside the rolled bill. Unroll the bill from around your thumb with the tip, and hand the bill out for examination.

TIPS

• Be sure that the thumb tip is not sitting too snugly on your thumb when you begin the effect; you'll want the tip to slide off freely.

• Removing the paper cork from the tube is an optional step; it merely makes the effect a little bit more intriguing.

• This effect works not only with with water, but also with sugar or salt!

PATTER

Here's an idea to work with: "It's not everything, but it's amazing what you can do with a little money...."

"When we do magic, we manipulate reality to create illusion. And when we do that, we make the impossible possible."
—Doug Henning

HOWARD FRANKLIN THURSTON
(1869-1936)

Thurston was born in Columbus, Ohio. In his twenties he began to study and work as a medical missionary, but one day in 1892, his career plans suddenly and irrevocably changed. En route to the University of Pennsylvania, he noticed a poster of Hermann the Great, a childhood idol. Thurston detoured and went to see the show. The next day, torn between his current path and the allure of magic, he cast his lot in favor of a performing career by boarding the same train as the Hermanns and silently following them to Syracuse.

At the peak of his career Thurston was the most famous magician in North America. In 1900 he began a world tour, but upon hearing that Kellar was preparing to name a successor, he rushed back to the States. In 1908 Kellar officially named Thurston as his successor. Thurston expanded Kellar's show, tripling it in size. He also perfected Kellar's famous levitation. In 1919 Thurston became the first magician to present a show on Broadway.

BILL TRANSPOSITION

Category
Transposition

Props
One thumb tip, one small drinking glass, a one dollar bill,
one paper towel or tissue, one rubber band

EFFECT

The magician covers the mouth of a small drinking glass with a paper towel. He secures it in place with a rubber band, giving it the appearance of a drumhead. The magician borrows a one dollar bill from a spectator and invites the spectator to mark the bill so that it can be identified later. The spectator marks the bill with symbols or with initials or in any other way that he chooses.

The magician folds the bill in half, four times, and then hands the tiny folded bill to the spectator to hold. The magician makes a fist, and assuring the spectator that it is empty, invites him to poke his finger down into the fist to confirm this fact for himself. The magician then takes the folded bill from the spectator and stuffs it down into his fist. He pronounces an incantation and then opens his hand. The bill has vanished.

The magician picks up the glass, which is covered with the paper towel. With his thumb he punctures a hole in the towel, reaches down into the glass, and produces a tightly folded bill. The magician hands it to the spectator. The spectator unfolds the bill; it is the original bill, the marked bill, the one that vanished.

SET-UP

Prior to presentation, place the thumb tip on your right thumb.

METHOD

Borrow a bill and have the spectator mark it. Take back the marked bill and hold it upright so that the picture of George Washington is facing the spectator **(fig. 1)**. You will now fold the bill a total of four times. First, fold the bill in half, from right to left. Second, fold it in half once again, from right to left. Third, fold it down, so that the top end meets the bottom end. Your fourth and last fold is again from top to bottom. You'll be left with a skinny folded bill, not more than the width of a finger. Hand the folded bill to the spectator to hold.

Make a fist with your left hand. Stick your right pointer into your left fist and say, "Would you please poke your finger into my fist and see for yourself that my fist is empty." After the spectator complies, your upcoming patter and action will provide the opportunity for a crucial move: As you say "You can see that it's definitely empty," simultaneously poke your right thumb into the fist, leaving the thumb tip behind. The words and action must be executed simultaneously, making it seem as if your action is merely an illustration of your words, and nothing more.

Take the folded bill from the spectator and place it into your left fist; the bill is secretly being inserted into the hidden thumb tip **(fig. 2)**. Using a different finger each time, casually poke the bill a couple of times, as though compressing it down into your fist. One of these pokes must, naturally, be with your right thumb, enabling you to insert your thumb into the tip and to remove the concealed bill from your left fist. Say your magic words. Open your fist. The bill appears to have vanished.

Poke your right thumb down through the paper towel that covers the water glass **(fig. 3)**. Leave the thumb tip

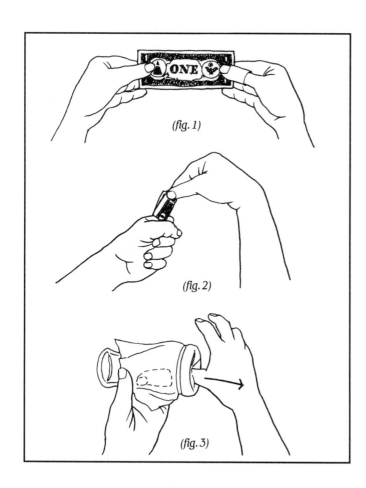

(fig. 1)

(fig. 2)

(fig. 3)

behind, inside the glass. Using a couple of fingers, withdraw the bill from the thumb tip, which remains concealed by the paper towel; the bill appears to come from inside the glass. Hand the bill to the spectator. It is clearly his original bill, the one with his personal markings.

TIPS

•When you drape the towel over the glass, it is very important that you have sufficient length to completely cover the sides of the glass so that the thumb tip remains concealed when you leave it behind!

•If you have excess toweling, you can twist the hanging length beneath the glass, completely enclosing the glass and creating a tight, packaged effect. Leave the glass lying on its side and pick it up when you are ready to puncture the towel and retrieve the bill.

•Don't actually compress the bill when pretending to poke it down into your left fist; slide your thumb into the tip right alongside the folded bill. The thumb tip will fit snugly.

Category
Restoration

Props
One thumb tip, two pieces of ribbon,
2 1/2" and 12" in length

EFFECT

The magician presents an ordinary piece of ribbon, about a foot long, and folds it in half. With a pair of scissors, he cuts the ribbon into two equal pieces and grabs the two cut ends in his fist. With his free hand, he takes hold of one of the ends of ribbon hanging down from his fist; the spectator is asked to hold the other. The magician blows on his fist. He opens it. The cut ribbon has been restored to one piece.

SET-UP

Take the 2 1/2" piece of ribbon and fold it in half, making a loop. Tape the two loose ends of ribbon into your thumb tip, leaving at least 1/2" of loop extending from the top **(fig. 1)**. Stick your right thumb into the thumb tip, pushing the entire loop into the tip as you do so. You are ready to present the effect when the tip is on your thumb, and the 2 1/2" of ribbon are hidden inside.

METHOD

Present the 12" ribbon and allow the spectator to inspect it. Fold the ribbon in half. With your left fist, grab the folded end of the ribbon. This folded end must be completely enclosed within your fist; the two loose ends hang visibly down from the bottom of your fist.

With your right thumb and pointer, reach into your left fist, as if intending to pull the hidden loop up into view.

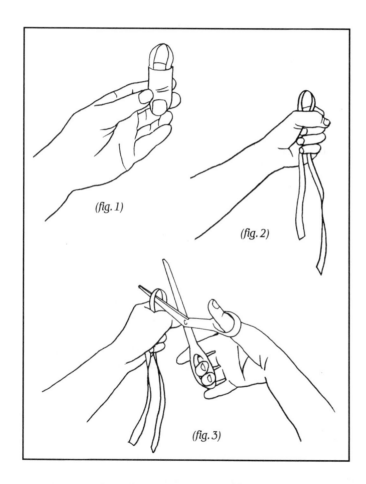

(fig. 1)

(fig. 2)

(fig. 3)

But secretly deposit the thumb tip in your left fist, and leave it there. Now pull the 2 1/2" loop up into view **(fig. 2)**. The spectator believes he is seeing the 12" ribbon. It is this small fake loop that is then cut in two **(fig. 3)**. It now appears as though there are two long lengths of ribbon hanging from your fist.

Push the two short, cut ends back into the thumb tip hidden in your fist, and push the tip back onto your right thumb. With your left fist, continue holding the 12" ribbon, which the spectator believes has been cut. Ask your spectator to grab one end, while you grab the other. Open your fist. The spectator expects to see two separate pieces, but the ribbon is whole. Take your bow.

"Remember what safes were made for — they were made to keep people out, not in."
—Bess Houdini, when asked how her husband
escaped from a locked safe

95

The

ARMCHAIR MAGICIAN

Three incredible stunts of
magical mental manipulation

MAGICIAN'S CHOICE

Category
Mentalism

Props
*Five different coins: a penny, a nickel, a dime,
a quarter, a half dollar*

EFFECT

The magician lays five coins side by side on the table. He says he will make a prediction, and on a small piece of paper he writes something down, folds the paper in half, and hands it to the spectator. The spectator is instructed to place the paper into his pocket without looking at it. The magician describes the "game" that is to follow. He tells the spectator that he will point to two coins. Of the two, the spectator will be asked to freely select one. The game begins.

The magician points to two coins, and the spectator selects one of the two. The magician pushes aside and eliminates the coin that the spectator has selected. The magician now tells the spectator that it is his turn to point to any two of the remaining coins that he likes. The magician now selects one of the two and that chosen coin is now eliminated. Once again it is the magician's turn to point to two coins. The spectator selects one of the two and that coin is pushed aside. Only two coins now remain.

The magician asks the spectator to push one of the two coins toward him. One coin now remains in the original lineup. The magician instructs the spectator to look at the prediction, which has been safely stored in his pocket. The paper is unfolded. The coin has been correctly predicted.

SET-UP

Make sure that five different coins are available for your use. No further set-up is required. The effect is repeatable.

METHOD

Make a decision as to which coin you'd like to predict (**fig. 1**). In our example we will use the dime. This effect works with the principle of Magician's Choice, so if using our example, throughout your performance you must never allow the dime to be eliminated. Whenever it is your turn to point to two coins it must never be the dime. When it's the spectator's turn to point to two coins, your choice must also never be the dime. Point to the other coin (**fig. 2**). When it's the spectator's turn to select two coins, he may never actually include the dime,

but if he does you will, of course, select the alternate coin (**fig. 3**).

You and the spectator will play the game back and forth until there are only two coins left. In our example, it will be the dime and some other coin. Ask the spectator to push one of the coins toward you (**fig. 4**). If he pushes that other coin toward you, eliminate it, leaving you with the predicted dime. If he pushes the dime toward you, still eliminate the other coin, leaving, once again, the dime.

A final note: The idea is always to impress upon the spectator that throughout the game he has total freedom of choice. In actuality you alone know that you've forced the dime on him by never giving him the opportunity to pick it, and you, in turn, never took advantage of picking it when it was offered to you.

TIPS

•It makes the effect more interesting if you don't line the coins up in denominational order: mix them up.

•If you wish to repeat the effect, you'll find that using other small objects such as marbles of different colors or playing cards works just as well. Master "Coin Prediction" and you'll be able to perform the effect whenever and wherever you wish. Our friend Joe, a carpenter, loves to perform this effect on the job, using washers, nuts, bolts, and nails. Be innovative, experiment.

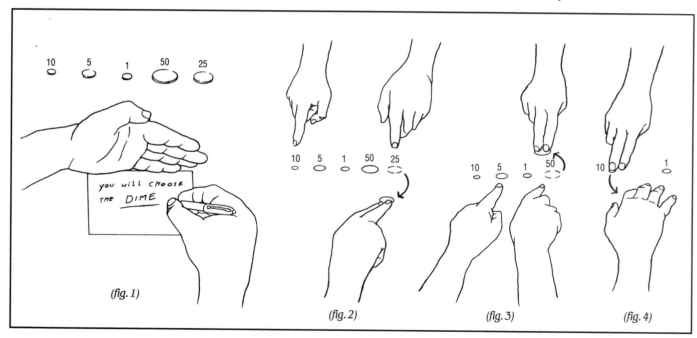

(fig. 1)   *(fig. 2)*   *(fig. 3)*   *(fig. 4)*

Category
Transposition

Prop
Cigarette ashes

EFFECT

The magician asks the spectator to extend his hands out in front of himself. The spectator is then told to choose one hand and to place the other, shut tightly in a fist, behind his back. The magician places a smudge of ashes on the top side of the spectator's extended hand. As he gently rubs it in, he asks the spectator if he feels the ashes penetrating his hand — does he feel them working their way through his body, all the way to his other arm, to his other hand? The magician asks the spectator to bring the hidden hand slowly out from behind his back. The spectator is told to turn his hand palm-up, and to release the fist. There is now a pronounced smudge of ash on the palm of the spectator's previously hidden hand; the cigarette ashes have traveled.

SET-UP

Secretly place a fair amount of ashes on the tips of the pointer and middle finger of your right hand.

METHOD

Ask your spectator to hold both his hands, palm down, out in front of himself. Whatever position he chooses, casually ask him to raise them a little higher. This is the key move of the effect. As you ask him to raise his hands, softly place your right thumb on top of his left hand, and your right pointer and middle finger on his palm; place your left thumb on top of his right hand, and your left pointer and middle finger on his palm. The ash-coated tips of your right hand are now lightly touching his left palm **(fig. 1)**. Your spectator believes you are merely adjusting the height of his hands. The move, casually executed, means absolutely nothing to him, and by the time the effect is completed, he can be counted on to have entirely forgotten that you ever touched him.

Ask your spectator to indicate one hand. If he chooses his right, ask him to place the other hand, the left, behind his back. If he chooses his left, ask him to place that hand behind his back. This exemplifies the principle of Magician's Choice. The spectator feels as though he is freely choosing, but no matter what he says, you will tell him to put his left hand behind his back and to leave the right extended.

Have him make a fist with the hidden left hand. Visibly place some cigarette ashes on your fingertips, and gently

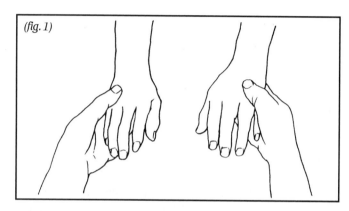

(fig. 1)

rub them onto the back of the spectator's extended right hand. For this effect, the patter is an essential component. It contributes to a Time Delay, putting an even greater distance between your crucial yet visible move and the surprise outcome of the trick. The intervening patter directs your spectator's attention to the tale you are weaving, creates suspense, and allows your key move to be ignored, to be taken for something unimportant, and amazing as it sounds, to be completely forgotten.

Ask the spectator to slowly bring out his left hand from behind his back. Instruct him to open his fist and look into his palm. The spectator witnesses the transposed ashes.

TIP

•While setting up this effect, don't be afraid to put a substantial amount of ash on your pointer and middle finger; you will never use too much.

PATTER

•You may wish to find an interesting pocket-size container in which to carry some ashes with you. Casually reveal the closed container to your spectator, then begin your story... "I once knew a woman who taught me about life. She was not only wise and good, she could do things the rest of us cannot. She could travel through space and time, will herself anywhere, alter events. I carry a bit of her ashes with me, now, wherever I go.... It reminds me of what's possible....

"I have a theory. Would someone help me with my experiment? Hold out your hands. A little higher." Place the hidden smudge on the participant's left palm. "Choose one hand. Place your left behind your back and make a fist.... I believe that even her ashes must hold a remnant of her extraordinary powers...." Visibly place a smudge on the participant's right hand. "Like her, the ashes won't be content to stay where they're placed, but will move of their own accord, through your body, and when they've finished exploring that which is invisible to the rest of us, will reemerge, elsewhere.... Quiet now. Concentrate. Do you feel enlightened in any way? Are you having any thoughts you never before had? Do you feel the ashes moving? Bring out your left fist. Open it." Pleased, indicate the ashes. "Ah, just as I thought..."

CARDINI (1894-1973)

Cardini was the first magician to create an act around the production of multiple card fans and lighted cigarettes. He was born Richard V. Pitchford in a Welsh fishing village. At seventeen he enlisted in the British army, perfecting his card fans in the World War I trenches. Because of the cold, he practiced while wearing a pair of gloves; the gloves later became his trademark. While convalescing from a war injury, he made his magic debut performing for other patients in the hospital. By the time he was discharged, his decision to become a professional magician had been made.

Cardini introduced the public to the craft of manipulation, elevating it to an art form.

THE MATING CARDS

Category
Revelation

Prop
One deck of cards

EFFECT

The magician presents two small piles of face-down cards, each pile containing twelve cards. The magician explains that each card has a mate. The two piles have been prearranged so that the first cards of each pile are mates, the second two are mates, the third cards are mates, etc. The magician demonstrates what he means by simultaneously turning up the top card of each pile and then, in turn, each successive card. In our example, he turns up two Red Nines, two Black Kings, two Black Jacks, two Red Fives, and so on. (It is irrelevent which cards from the full deck the magician has chosen for the effect.)

After showing all the cards, the magician turns both piles face-down. The magician picks up one of the two piles and says that he is now going to mix up the cards in a simple fashion; he will randomly deal some of the cards straight down onto the table, and he will sometimes randomly reverse a card with the card just behind it before dealing them both down onto the table.

After he has mixed the pile in what appears to be a random fashion, he again, simultaneously, turns up the top card of each pile and then, one at a time, each successive card on both piles. The two piles are no longer in their mated order; clearly, the chosen pile has been mixed.

The magician again turns both piles face-down. He picks up the pile that hasn't yet been mixed and now asks the spectator to assist him in shuffling them by deciding for the magician which cards should be dealt straight down onto the table, and which cards should have their position reversed with the adjacent cards. The spectator is allowed to make each decision as the magician makes his way through the entire pile.

The magician is now ready to show the spectator the result of his choices. The top card of each pile is turned face-up. It is a match! Each successive card of both piles is turned up; both piles are once again perfectly mated, two Red Nines, two Black Kings, and so on, twelve pairs of matched cards.

SET-UP

It makes no difference which twenty-four cards you decide to use as long as you have twelve pairs of mates, two Black Eights, two Red Aces, two Black Threes, etc.

Prearrange the two piles of twelve so that each card in your first pile is in the same position as its mate in the second pile. Present them, face-down, in this order, to your spectator.

METHOD

Explain to your spectator that each card in each pile has a mate. Reveal all twenty-four cards by simultaneously turning over the top card of each pile and then, in turn, each successive card of each pile. The two piles are shown to be in mated order (**fig. 1**).

Turn both piles face-down. With your left hand, pick up either one of the piles and tell your spectator that you are now going to give the cards a simple mix. As you say, "I can deal some cards straight down onto the table," use your right hand to deal two or three cards down onto the table. Continue by saying, "... or I can reverse the order of some of the cards by switching a card with the one behind it." But this time, you will not be doing exactly what you say you are; as you make this latter statement, you will employ a very simple, but deceptive move.

While still holding the pile in your left hand, slide off the top card into your right hand, but do not put it down. Push off the next card from the pile that's in your left hand, and place it on top of the card you're holding in your right fingertips (**fig. 2**). Place them both down,

as they are, onto the previously dealt cards from that pile on the table.

You will find that if you practice this move until you are able to do it without hesitation, it will truly look as though

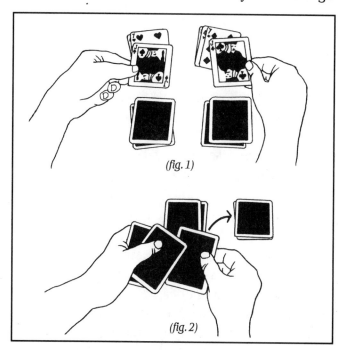

(fig. 1)

(fig. 2)

you are reversing the deck. In actuality, nothing has happened; the previous order has been maintained. This move is called a "reverse." Perform it randomly by, for example, first dealing a few straight down, then doing a reverse or two, then again dealing straight down. It will absolutely look as though you are thoroughly mixing the cards.

After completing this false shuffle, flip up all the cards in both piles, one pair at a time. They no longer match. But remember, the cards are not really mixed. The reason they no longer match is simply because you have taken one pile and have reversed the entire pile's order, as a whole. In private, take a look, and you'll see that the bottom card of one pile is a mate to the top card of your other pile!

After showing your spectator that the pile has been "mixed," scoop up both piles and, once again, turn them face-down. Pick up the pile that wasn't mixed, and ask the spectator to assist you in mixing them by allowing him to tell you which cards he wants dealt straight down and which ones he wants you to reverse. Whenever he says "reverse," remember to take the card into your right fingertips, put the next card from the pile in your left

hand on top of it, and place them, in this order, onto the table. Whenever he says "straight down," do exactly as he has asked.

When you've completed the whole pile of twelve, simultaneously turn over both piles of cards, one card at a time. The cards are once again in order, mate matching mate. You might wish to conclude by saying that "playing cards are much like people; they always find their mate."

TIPS

•Another interesting way to present this effect is to take your business cards, or, if you don't have any, to use index cards, and to draw twelve pairs of matching shapes on them. Use a circle, square, triangle, star, a circle inside a square, a dot inside a triangle, etc. Drum up different combinations; use your imagination and you won't run out of shapes.

•This is a great little trick that lends itself to lots of entertaining patter. As you can see, you don't have to limit yourself to playing cards; some magicians create engaging routines about the mystery of destiny with the use of tarot cards.

BRAVO! ENCORE!

Before we take our leave, we'd like to present you with some last-minute pointers and a few gentle reminders. We'll begin with a little practical advice....

SOME TIPS ON PRACTICE

Every successful magician will have his or her own opinion regarding how a novice should practice the craft. We all agree that you should practice as much as possible, but unlike some of our colleagues, we fervently believe that the best way to perfect your newfound craft is to practice almost immediately on friends and family, not in private and not in front of a mirror. Don't wait until your method is perfected. Guaranteed, you'll make some mistakes, but don't worry about it. What you'll learn about your technique, what works and what doesn't, could never be learned in private nor could it ever be taught. Your hands-on experience will prove to be invaluable. A further suggestion is to practice your moves while you're engaged in other unrelated activities, while you're on the telephone or watching television. Your goal is to have your moves become second nature to you, to be able to execute them without concentrating. In addition, your object as a magician is to move naturally and normally. The human mind analyzes only that which it thinks it doesn't understand. It will not analyze, it will unquestionably accept that which it considers to be normal. Therefore, the more natural your mannerisms, words, and movements, the less your spectator's mind will notice or question them. Executed naturally and casually, even the most vital action of a trick, the move that enables the entire effect to work, will be accepted, overlooked, and forgotten. The satisfied mind will not try to interpret what it sees; it will not question. Your object as the magician is to satisfy your spectator's mind with normal, natural physical actions.

EENIE, MEENIE, CHILE BEANIE; THE SPIRITS ARE ABOUT TO SPEAK
or Performing for Children

We consider children, up to about the age of twelve, to be a separate and special group. The best effects to perform are simple and colorful. Children, in general, are usually unimpressed with card tricks; they're unable to distinguish one card from another.

Tricks such as "The Color-Changing Thimble" and "The Mystical Silk" are best for the very young; the child finds them as miraculous as the adult does. Adapt your patter appropriately, and don't overlook the supreme power of magical language...hocus-pocus, abracadabra, sim sa la bim, alakazam.... As corny and overdone as these words may seem, they're appealing and still meaningful to the very young, as well as to their very mature parents. Making up your own words and rhymes can be great fun, as well.

THE THUMB TIP

The prop you have received with *The Armchair Magician* was selected because of its great versatility and the ease with which it will enable you to perform extraordinary magic effects. The thumb tip is practical; it's easy to keep on your person at any time, and it never wears out. Despite its apparent simplicity, the thumb tip is actually a very serious piece of apparatus that is used by professional magicians throughout the world.

We do not exaggerate about the supreme versatility and popularity of this ancient device. Unfortunately, it is a device that is usually misunderstood by the beginner. It looks far too phoney, they believe, to fool anybody. We ask that you put aside your skepticism for just a few moments, and allow us to show you the surprising capabilities of this tool, and the incredible fun you will have learning to use it.

Let's begin by placing the thumb tip on your right thumb, your left, if you prefer. You'll probably notice that it does not match your skin color very well. (If it does, you need to get more sun.) All kidding aside, it makes no difference whether it matches or not; the color will in no way either hinder or help your performance.

Now that the thumb tip is on, walk up to a mirror, and make believe you are going to show an audience that your hands are empty. There is no need to stretch out your fingers or to hold them wide apart to prove your point. Just relax both of your hands, and aim your fingertips out toward your audience. Now look at your image in the mirror; the thumb tip is hardly noticeable. Imagine how invisible it would appear to an audience that doesn't know that such a prop even exists! While performing, do not look at the thumb tip; pay no attention to it. Forget that you're even wearing it. Just relax, and in all the tricks that you learn, it will always go undetected. With this device, you will be able to vanish lit cigarettes, produce small silks, vanish and produce sugar, salt, water, and perform countless other miracles.

The earliest thumb tips were made of wax, leather, or metal, then painted a flesh color. We do not know for sure how far back in time they actually go, but we have seen them mentioned in magic books that are more than one hundred years old. Through the decades, magicians have come up with all sorts of new clever magic devices, but the simple thumb tip has never been abandoned or replaced.

We cannot say enough about the effectiveness of this device. Everything in magic takes a little practice, the thumb tip being no exception. But eighty per cent of the task is in knowing that it will work. So don't be nervous, and enjoy the numerous ways in which you'll be doing what looks like the truly miraculous.

DO'S AND DON'TS

Do practice all your tricks before performing them.

Don't let on if you make a mistake; pretend it was intentional. Your audience doesn't know exactly what you were planning to do, anyway.

Do master only a few effects at a time. Learn the two or three that appeal to you the most; avoid trying to learn too much too quickly.

Don't ever immediately repeat a trick; your spectator will now know what to look for.

Do leave your audience wanting more; learning when to stop is an art in itself.

Don't allow hecklers to spoil your act; it's best to ignore them.

Do remember to suit your patter to your audience; the adult can appreciate the child's world, the child cannot appreciate the adult's.

Don't give in to your spectator's unrelenting curiosity; a true magician never reveals the secret!

You now possess knowledge that has been a long-guarded secret in the ancient fraternity of magicians. You're beginning to understand basic, fundamental principles like Misdirection and False Assumption. You're discovering that many, many tricks are not quite as difficult as you once imagined.

Pick your favorite effects; we hope you'll master all of them. But always remember that it's important not to just do the magic, it's essential to *believe* in it. Finally, the most important rule of all — have fun! And you'll find yourself truly working magic...in your life and in every life you touch.

Break a leg!

For Further Reading

The following books can be found through your local magic dealer, or directly from the publisher.

Bobo, J. B. **Modern Coin Magic.** Chicago, IL: Magic Inc.

Corinda. **13 Steps to Mentalism**. Brooklyn, NY: D. Robbins & Co.

Hugard, Jean. **The Royal Road to Card Magic**. London, England: Faber & Faber.

Rice, Harold R. **Rice's Encyclopedia of Silk Magic.** Boston, MA: ESM Publishers, Inc.

Tarbell, Dr. Harlan. **The Tarbell Course in Magic.** Brooklyn, NY: D. Robbins & Co.

For Magic Supplies

Abracadabra
10 Christopher St.
New York, NY 10014

Al's Magic Shop
1012 Vermont Ave. N.W.
Washington, DC 20005

Daytona Magic
136 South Beach St.
Daytona Beach, FL 32114

Hank Lee's Magic Factory
125 Lincoln Street
Boston, MA 02111

Hollywood Magic
6614 Hollywood Blvd.
Hollywood, CA 90028

Magic, Inc.
5082 N. Lincoln Ave.
Chicago, IL 60255

Steven's Magic Emporium
3238 East Douglas
Wichita, KS 67208

WANT TO BE A PART OF
THE WORLD OF MAGIC?

Mail a self-addressed stamped business envelope to:

Conjurer's Crew, The Magic Company
P.O. Box 2207
New York, NY 10009

We'll send you the most current news about the world of magic, from David Copperfield to Siegfried and Roy, along with information about the latest technological advances. With your first newsletter you will also receive a bonus magic trick to help expand your repertoire. And please feel free to tell us more about yourselves and your interest in magic. We'd love to hear from you.

Remember: Magic is easy, magic is fun, magic is real!